VOICES OF CHANGE

VOICES
OF
CHANGE

IMMIGRANT WRITERS SPEAK OUT

Edited by Jurgen Hesse

PULP PRESS
Vancouver

VOICES OF CHANGE
Copyright © 1990 by Jurgen Hesse

Published by:
PULP PRESS BOOK PUBLISHERS
100-1062 Homer Street
Vancouver, B.C. Canada V6B 2W9
A Division of Arsenal Pulp Press Book Publishers Ltd.

COVER DESIGN: David Lester
PHOTO CREDITS: Eva Busza (Andrew Busza); Rafael
  Goldchain (Alberto Manguel); Zarov (Anna Sandor);
  Ian Smith (Jim Wong-Chu)
PRINTING: Hignell Printing
TYPESETTING: Vancouver Desktop Publishing Centre
PRINTED AND BOUND IN CANADA

CANADIAN CATALOGUING IN PUBLICATION DATA:
Main entry under title:
Voices of change

  ISBN 0-88978-221-0

  1. Authors, Canadian (English) – 20th century – Interviews.
2. Immigrants – Canada – Interviews. I. Hesse, Jurgen.
PS8089.5.I45V64 1990   C810'.9'0054   C90-091211-1
PR9188.2.I45V64.1990

ACKNOWLEDGEMENTS

My gratitude goes first to the Department of the Secretary of State, Multiculturalism, for having assisted me generously with a working grant. My special appreciation is for Linda Field who worked on my book and found its weak spots unerringly. Then I thank my good friend and fellow-writer John Munro for his practical help and advice. I also thank Jim Wong-Chu, who passed along the names of a number of immigrant writers whom I included in this book. I owe gratitude to Brian Lam, my publisher, who saw the value of such a book in about ten seconds and trusted me to deliver. Then I must thank Mary Lastoria, who transcribed the interviews, for her immaculate job. And naturally, my thanks to the writers who contributed to this book.

CONTENTS

INTRODUCTION

The fifteen immigrant writers in this collection of interviews come from a number of diverse locales: Europe, Latin America, Hong Kong and the Punjab region of India. Despite such differences, they all have in common the fact that their immigrant experience is central to their work, whether they are "writers from different cultures writing in English," as Norbert Ruebsaat puts it, or whether they still write in their first language.

The book, then, is based on nothing more than a hunch that immigrant writers' voices are ones of change. They speak about their love for Canada, their troubles with the lack of a literary milieu, issues like hidden racism and active discrimination, the slow and agonizing process of acculturation, and discovering who their audience is. As well, I hoped that these interviews would give the reader a notion of what we immigrant writers feel, and how we express our reaction to our host country. I believe the resulting collection of interviews is the first attempt in Canadian literature to give voice to a specific group of writers.

Not being an academic myself, but rather a lifelong professional writer, I hesitate to draw conclusions vis-a-vis Canadian literature. I have questions, but lack an overview, so I turned to a man whose judgment and expertise I trust, Ron Hatch, who teaches in the English Department at the University of British Columbia. Following are excerpts from an interview with Dr. Hatch.

JURGEN HESSE: What is this thing, Canadian literature?

RON HATCH: People often define it in opposition to American literature. When the U.S. had its revolution in 1776, the founding of a new nation, in fact there were two nations founded at that point, something which most Canadians know. But not the Americans— they see it only as one nation. One being very individualistic, extraordinarily liberal, being the American, and the other being very conservative, very loyalist, the individual looking to the country to fulfill himself/herself through the country. That would be Canada. Often you find in Canadian literature, as opposed to American literature, that the American will take off for the territories, where the (Canadian) Indian heads out at the end of the book. Whereas in Canada there is frequently a sense of returning home, of leaving for a short time. Then, in order to fulfill the individual, he will return home again.

What is this home?

Family, community, and the larger nation. That would be defining Canada in terms of its not being the United States. That has been a large dimension right from the beginning.

Norbert Ruebsaat states very emphatically in his interview that the English, the Anglo-Saxons, were just as much immigrants as were the Europeans who followed later. That the original Canadians were the native people.

That's something it has taken Canadians a long time to come to. There was a recent article in *The Beaver,* in which the author talked about Alexander Mackenzie's "guided tour to the Pacific," that Mackenzie in fact was guided all the way through a very populous area, and that in those moments when he lost his guides, or the guides left him, he was helpless. That what he was doing was not moving through a land that had not been written on or wasn't cultivated, but moving through villages, trapping and hunting areas that were very well known to the Indians. Articles like that have changed the perspective enormously to include the First Peoples, because almost all of our early literature, up to the fifties, maybe even the sixties, ignored this fact and saw the British and the French and all the other nationalities who came here to a land that was uninhabited, that the Indians were not being taken account of. That begins to change, to some extent, with writers like Duncan Campbell Scott who writes about the Métis people around the turn of the century. Pauline Johnson (she was half Indian herself, her father was a chief) begins to make that change. It's really noticeable with Howard O'Hagan's *Tête Jaune,* and then a big novel by Rudy Wiebe, *The Temptations of Big Bear,* in 1973, which won the Governor

General's Award. It takes you inside the Indian mind, but Howard O'Hagan does it as well. Rudy Wiebe gives you two narrative streams—the white narrative being entirely linear—and the Big-Bear-Cree-Indians narrative with a powerful circular sense there.

Believable?

Very believable, very powerful novel. Some people have claimed it was the best novel ever written in Canada. Steven Parmenius, a Hungarian who came over with Sir Humphrey Gilbert in the 16th century and travelled to Newfoundland with Sir Humphrey and was shipwrecked there, talked about coming to find the land of gold: it's that old image of a golden world before the fall. He hardly set foot on Newfoundland and wrote a poem about it in Latin, about his feelings, about the possibility of finding a new world here that would be golden. This has always been one of the ideals of the immigrant writer—the immigrant generally—when he comes, that he would find a world different from the old class-ridden world. Many of the immigrants, especially if they weren't English or Scottish, came here to escape the terrible conditions they had endured in Europe.

There's a group of writers in Canada who came up with that wonderful phrase—I'm sure that it must have originated in California—structural racism, by which dictum Rudy Wiebe had no business writing about Indians because he is a Mennonite-Canadian. What does he know about native Indians. How valid is that dictum?

There's been a lot of talk about that recently, and you probably know about the debate that's been raging between Wiebe and W.P. Kinsella in the *Globe and Mail*. Wiebe claimed that Kinsella has been victimizing the Indians on the Hobbema Reserve, and Kinsella responded that he can write about any bloody thing he wants, that his books sell, and that's all that matters to him. Wiebe argued that Kinsella doesn't know enough about the Indians, and Kinsella agrees. Wiebe implied that when he wrote about the Indians, he spent an enormous amount of time researching them, trying to get it as right as he could, and to tell their story. Kinsella simply wants to tell amusing stories. Wiebe is perhaps not arguing from a structural racist point of view but taking the point that many Indian writers have taken, that "if you're going to write about us, you had better do it in an authentic way."

It depends on how it's done.

Right. The proof will be in how well you do it. At one of the recent writers' meetings there was an Indian writer who seemed to be arguing for a while that no whites should write about Indians, and a white writer asked, "Are you telling me I can't do that?" and the Indian writer said, "No, but you do it at your own peril."

When I came here in 1958 from Germany, Canadian literature was not something I was looking for. I had been reading many of the important writers in German, English, French, Russian, Italian and American literature, but Canadian writers were not among them. I harbored a kind of superiority complex, as Ruebsaat calls it. Was that attitude justified? Was there not much of Canadian literature in the fifties?

No, a lot was starting to happen then. The oldest tradition in Canada is the poetic tradition. You can date the poetry well back into the 19th century, and partly that was simply because it was much easier for an individual to write and publish poems. The poetry begins first, the novel comes second, but in fact most people date the beginning of the serious Canadian novel from the 1920s, 1930s, and even the 1940s, with books like *Barometer Rising* (Hugh MacLennan), and *The Tin Flute* by Gabriel Roy. But the first novel written in the new land was written about what is now Canada, and that was in 1769, *The History of Emily Montague* by Frances Brooke, very soon after the Treaty of Paris in 1763. The people in the book were English people using Canada as an exotic backdrop.

    People often say that Canadian literature is discovered every twenty years, every new generation, and there was a big movement in the late twenties, and then another in the mid-forties, to create a Canadian voice, to speak in a Canadian voice about Canadian problems. This carries all the way through the fifties. Frequently the people at this time tried to take publishing into their own hands. They were very strongly left-wing, ant-Fascist, anti-Franco, anti-Duplessis in Quebec. By the fifties, there developed a strong literary movement in Canada. But even at that time, MacLennan noted that serious readers always looked to American reviews, because Canadians didn't trust themselves or Canadian literature, and it wasn't until the book was praised abroad that, in fact, it was taken seriously here.

And the next discovery of Canadian literature was in the mid-sixties?

Yes, you find a lot of the big writers at that time, Margaret Laurence developing a very large following in Canada, one of the most beloved of all Canadian writers. And then the movement grew out here to the west coast. There was the importation of the Black Mountain poetry (from the United States) through Warren Tallman at UBC. (George) Woodcock is arriving in this period. *Prism Magazine* is growing, contemporary verse is growing. But you would still not find many Canadian literature courses at universities in the sixties, that only takes place as a result of student demand. It was not until the late sixties/early seventies that Canadian literature was being taken seriously.

What is the role of the non-British immigrant writer in Canadian literature?

There are the two founding languages in Canada, and if you were taking a course in Canadian literature in the English department, you would also do some French-Canadian literature. Now, in the eighties, you really began to feel the impact of other people starting to write about their nationality. We already had Frederick Philip Grove, that displaced German Felix Paul Berthold Friedrich Greve. He came over in the early teens and became a school teacher in Manitoba in 1913. He invented a whole new personality for himself, a new name, and wrote a large number of novels under the name of Frederick Philip Grove. It was only discovered fairly recently that he was Felix Paul Berthold Friedrich Greve. He knew people like André Gide, tried to make his living in Germany, fell into debt, had women problems, and eventually just disappeared, faked his death, and like the old man in Günter Grass's *The Tin Drum,* just turned up with a new name and started writing. He said he was born in Sweden, and people accepted it. Now there's a German who came over and wrote about communities, often with German-Scandinavian characters. He really described the opening-up of the West.

A literary immigrant pioneer.

Exactly, and of course he came with a strong writer background, having met many major figures of the day in Europe. Novels like *Fruits of the Earth, Settlers of the Marsh,* very biblical titles, and he sees these men as giants, overcoming tremendous odds, at the same time becoming moral failures. None of their energies went into creating, for themselves, character. They frequently lose their families even as they build a magnificent farm for the family. He describes that tradition in Canada, the man giving himself over to building the nation, as it were, but not having anything left for himself and for his family.

Let's go back to the impact of the immigrant writers in the eighties.

Often it's not just the immigrant writers. You have people like Jan Drabek writing here in B.C. But (there are) also other people who have been here for many generations and are suddenly discovering that it's important that they write about their own Icelandic community, for example. Now the Jews have done that already: Mordecai Richler and Adele Wiseman. Aritha Van Herk is interested in that as well, and Rudy Wiebe, with his Mennonite novels in the sixties. Then the native peoples as well, like Jeannette Armstrong, have been writing about their community from the inside.

What upsets some English and French Canadians is that Canada looks as though it were becoming more multicultural, not simply remain the two founding nations with two separate languages, but all these different nations. For instance Joy Kogawa writing about the Japanese experience in the internment camps, and her poetry. You can't look anymore just to the two founding nations and languages, but at the different communities in the country, and they all seem to come up with their own writers. There's a strong sense that Canada is moving toward a multicultural paradigm, rather than a two-nation paradigm.

Dr. Hatch and I did not discuss another Canadian phenomenon which began to make itself felt in the mid-sixties: cultural nationalism. The practitioners of this cultural nationalism, primarily dedicated to lessening or even demolishing the strong cultural influence of the Americans and in turn creating a distinct Canadian culture (whatever that may be), often became strident in their attitutdes and came close to being cultural chauvinists.

Cultural nationalism, whatever its merits and demerits, is some-what distant to the thinking of many immigrant Canadian writers. Speaking for myself, and no doubt for many other European im-migrants, I shudder every time one of my Canadian friends tells me he or she is a nationalist. For me a nationalist is pure anathema, a totalitarian vision to eschew at all costs, whether with or without the adjective "cultural." We Europeans were stung by a nationalism gone berserk, and we cannot easily abide intelligent, social-democratic Canadians proclaiming for nationalism. I, for my part, call myself a dedicated internationalist, culturally, economically, and politically speaking. I am saddened when my nationalist Canadian writer friends inevitably draw the erroneous conclusion that ergo, I must be a conservative, or worse, a reactionary. Let me tell them: We have other scores to settle, other preoccupations, other areas to explore, other skeletons in the closet. American cultural dominance is not of crucial importance to some of us. We like to think that a strong Canadian culture will evolve not by Canadian writers (whether born here or outside Canada) being cultural nationalists but by producing strong works. One example of how it can be done is Australian cinema, which has acquired a reputation for quality beyond national origin.

I was born in Wuppertal-Vohwinkel, Germany, in 1924. In my first seven years I became fluently bilingual, speaking German at home, Italian in Italian school, German in the German school in Turin, and Italian on the street with other Italian boys.

Our stay in Italy was to be cut short by dramatic events. First, father died of chronic nephritis in 1930. After father's death, mother had taken up with an Italian and—as it turned out—an adulterer. In those days adultery was a criminal offence, and one morning two *carabinieri* arrested him and mother.

For a week my older sister and I were temporarily orphaned and were taken in, among wagging tongues in the neighborhood, by two German families. The scandal! German widow in gaol for adultery with a no-good Italian! The *judice istruttore* (investigating magistrate) was lenient and mother was released. Her plans for opening an elegant tea room for the blasé nouveaux riche in Monte Carlo fell apart. After having sold everything we owned in two days, the three of us boarded a train for southern Bavaria where mother had friends.

I felt like a fugitive on this trip, egged on in this belief by my mother's panic. She thought the *carabinieri* would be back and once again detain her. I remember arriving in the Allgäu region at the age of ten, filled with fantasies of pursuit and derring-do. There, mother opened a *Fremdenheim*, a guest house for Germans and British visitors.

In this peasant village, which was already destined to become one of the desirable vacation spas in Bavaria, I went to high school, catching up on my interrupted education. I was no longer left alone, as I had been in Italy, for in Germany—after all, it was 1935 and Hitler had an iron hold on all Germans' destinies—I was expected to attend Hitler Youth meetings, wearing my brown shirt and shorts, singing and marching, listening to political indoctrination.

I was not, however, an altogether good German boy. Rebelliousness against any kind of authority and social or political pressure seemed inbred, and always I felt superior to the other local boys who seemed to drift, like the Gadarene swine, into mindless obeisance and submission. Not I, the semi-orphaned son of a powerful Prussian from the grande bourgeoisie. But these were only dreams of rebellion; in reality I also drifted along with the others. Rebellion was reserved for high school in Oberstdorf, where I was told bluntly by my German teacher that "one thing is clear, Jürgen, you'll never be a writer." That dire prediction, coupled with generally poor marks, made me quit school at seventeen and go to work in a factory where, one day, I might soar to the dizzying heights of *Prokurist*, or executive vice-president.

Two things interfered with this dismal future. Three months before I was to be drafted at age eighteen, in 1942, I fell ill and nearly died from rheumatic fever and other complications which left me weak and with a poor heart. That heart condition most likely saved my life, for it prevented service in the Wehrmacht. I had never wanted to be a soldier. And, the war ended.

I remember it well. On April 27th, 1945, we were targets for Allied bombs and bullets. On April 28th, we were "liberated" by the

French occupation forces which, six weeks later, were replaced by the U.S. Army. With the U.S. Army came opportunity. Soon I worked for an officers club washing glasses, later dispensing drinks behind the bar, finally advancing to assistant club manager.

Any thoughts of chronicling those last days of Hitler and the early days of French General de Lattre de Tassigny and General Eisenhower vanished while I absorbed the American presence in Bavaria and wolfed down any spare food available in those three lean years after the war. I learned English from the G.I. Joes. English was by then my fourth language.

By 1948 I spoke English more or less fluently, and when I met two Quaker women who worked as voluntary relief workers in Ludwigshafen for the American Friends Service Committee, I visited the mission and asked to become an extracurricular relief worker. The nine months with the Quakers not only replaced my army slang with more literary English—the Quakers were mostly university graduates—but created in me a deep desire to write. When the Quakers left Germany in the spring of 1949, I took a job with the Amerika Haus in Mannheim across the river, a library-cum-cultural-activities centre operated by the U.S. Information Service.

At the age of twenty-four, I started reading world literature in English translation, systematically and voraciously. I also began to write. A novel—what else—a tale of an idealistic teacher who is trying to save a village from destruction and who gets vilified by capitalist interests. It was a very bad novel, full of clichés and cardboard characters moving in a landscape of grey disasters.

The long arm of Senator Joe McCarthy extended all the way to Mannheim in 1951, when I was fired from the Amerika Haus due to an order from Army G-2 (intelligence) in Stuttgart. To this day, I have not been able to discover what my political crime (or misdemeanor) had been, despite the U.S. Freedom of Information Act. Being made into a political alien was quite traumatic. Although I felt rather honored for being thought a security risk, the long-range effect was less exhilarating. The slime, as I saw it, of unjustified political persecution leaves its mark on all of its victims. I took time off to finish my novel, and through a chance contact with Jean Cau, the secretary of Jean-Paul Sartre, I was given a chance to go to

Hamburg to present my novel to the editor-in-chief of the famous Rowohlt Verlag, Hans Ledig-Rowohlt.

The rejection, when it came, was a much worse blow than being fired by the Americans. I gave up writing fiction. Perhaps my German teacher had been right, after all. I started drifting from job to job until a postcard arrived in Frankfurt where I was working as an Air France sales representative. My friend Wilhelm Herrmann offered me a steady freelance job as reporter-at-large with the *Rhein-Neckar Zeitung*. I moved to Mannheim, and two days later I turned in my first feature. At the age of thirty, I had found my vocation.

My love for writing had shifted from fiction (after the novel had followed a large number of short stories, a ballet script, and a film script which a friend and I turned into an underground avant-garde film) to non-fiction, at which I was doing much better. Four years later, in 1958, I was finally accepted by the immigration authorities in Canada. An attempt in 1952 to immigrate to Canada had been rejected, thanks to Senator McCarthy's efficient intervention. Now I was ready to leave Germany, this time with a solid profession and four languages.

Canada was hard at first. The *Vancouver Sun* told me I ought to perfect my English before trying a career as a reporter. I couldn't argue with them, for I had not yet written anything in English. Three years went by. Then the *Province* contracted a series of six features on immigrants in Vancouver. I was both elated and terrified, but once I started writing in English, the features took shape and were printed. I had made that broad jump from writing in my native language to writing in my fourth language successfully. That was in 1961, and in 1963 the Toronto *Globe and Mail* hired me as a staff writer.

Pure paradise. Parallel to writing in English came my freelance career as a radio documentarist for the Canadian Broadcasting Corporation, one of the best radio networks in the world. Even after I moved back to Vancouver in 1966, I continued with the CBC, putting out radio documentaries and radio stereo features in large numbers. This medium of radio was more satisfying than writing for newspapers, more inspiring and more creative, involving not only research, interviews, and writing, but also recording sound effects and music, and finally packaging the product in a studio with staff producer and technician.

In the early days of my radio work, I was able to sell a short story to the program for which John Drainie read. I had finally made it in fiction as well, in a modest way. But writing books eluded me until, in 1985, the CBC killed almost all of its hour-long radio documentaries, leaving me without my bread-and-butter income. So I turned to writing books and learned to live more frugally than before.

In 1985 I self-published *The Story of ACTRA* (Alliance of Canadian Cinema and Television Artists), and in 1987 two self-help books were published by International Self-Counsel Press, *The Radio Documentary Handbook* and the *Mobile Retirement Handbook*. In 1988 followed the self-published *Tips & Tools for Better Writing*. By 1987, I had also finished writing what I call a documentary novel about a young German who grows up in Nazi Germany and is neither an underground hero nor a fellow-traveller. I am still sitting on the manuscript.

Whether the first-generation immigrant writer from a non-English culture will ever become a part of mainstream literature is uncertain at best. Discovering Canadian reality through immigrant eyes is a literary experience of the first magnitude, and these writers are, without exception, writing about Canada. If anything, my hope for this book is for it to be a more accurate portrait of the changing face of Canadian literature as we know it, thereby legitimizing the multiplicity of cultures at the heart of Canadian writing life.

—J.H.

Sadhu
Binning

Sadhu Binning was born in Punjab, India, in 1947, and immigrated to Canada in 1967. Until recently, he conclusively wrote in his native language, Punjabi, but, encouraged by friends, he has tried to write in English. His poetry and fiction have appeared in most of the major Punjabi literary journals published in Punjab and abroad. He has also published a book of poetry (1976) and a collection of short stories (1982). In 1986 he co-edited an anthology of Canadian-Punjabi poetry. He was the editor of a literary magazine, *Watno Dur*, from 1977 to 1982, and assistant editor for two years prior to that. Currently he is the co-editor for *Watan*, a literary and cultural quarterly.

Some of his English poems have appeared in *Canadian Dimension, Toronto South Asian Review, Labour/Le Travail, Minnesota Review*, and *5 A.M.* His work has also appeared in two poetry anthologies.

For the last few years he has been involved with a Punjabi theatre group, Vancouver Sath, in Vancouver. During this period he co-authored (with a fellow Sath member) and directed seven plays dealing with the problems of the Indo-Canadian community. Two of these plays, *Picket Line* and *A Crop of Poison*, were translated by the authors and produced in English as well. He lives in Vancouver, B.C.

"I believe that literature, like other matters in life, must serve a purpose. If I'm struggling against inequalities, injustices, and racism in my daily life, then my writing should also reflect this struggle."

JURGEN HESSE: I would like to know a little bit about your background, where you were born, what your early experiences were.

SADHU BINNING: I was born in Punjab, India, and I had my basic education there. High school.

What language did you speak?

I spoke Punjabi, but in school we also learned Hindi, and from grade six on we also learned English. So now I know four languages.

What is the fourth?

Urdu. Which is the official language of Pakistan now. And before the British occupation of that part of the world, Urdu was the main language used in the official circles.

Are you fluent in all four?

Yes I am.

I have no idea what kind of childhood experiences a man like you would have. How strong are your native influences?

As far as my personal life within my house is concerned, I would say very strong. My tastes are the same. I like literature, folk literature, and when I was young in high school, I liked watching Hindi films. I still do. I still enjoy that.

Here you live sort of two lives. One is within the four walls that you are living in, and the second, outside. I think I have probably lost quite a bit because it is a big change coming from India. You know, there are a lot of changes one has to make. How you meet people. For example, the concept of friendship is totally different where I come from. Here when you meet people a friendship sometimes means different things.

Well, here you make friends immediately, and then you lose sight of them and they are gone.

Right, and the feeling is not that strong. Maybe it is my personal experience, but I have some friends from childhood days that are very close still. Whether we meet occasionally or regularly, we have very strong ties, and I have known a lot of other people. It doesn't matter how often you meet them, or how close you become. There is still that lack of sort of closeness that I felt (in the Punjab). So it is things like that. Some of the things I am quite happy to lose. When in India, where some people don't lose it, they are very sort of stuck up.

I still think there are a lot of things—after being here twenty-two years—which I miss. A lot of things, I don't know if I could still have them in India if I was there, but some of those things I miss here.

Tell me about your writing. What was the first thing you wrote, other than in school, and in what language?

It was in Punjabi, and I wrote it when I was here in Canada. I came here in 1967, and when I came there weren't too many (Indo-Canadian) people here. The society was just beginning to increase in numbers. In the sixties the numbers were still small, and it was in the early seventies when it began. So when I came here I didn't have too many friends, Indo-Canadian or Punjabi. My English was not that good, so I could not go out and make friends. And, when you come from a different culture, there are a lot of hesitations and fears.

I think it was a kind of loneliness I felt, even when I worked in a sawmill in North Vancouver where there were a lot of other Punjabi workers. But even with those I felt quite lonely, and from that loneliness I think something began to take shape inside. I would start murmuring some song, sort of. You know. Eventually it became something that I have been calling poetry.

At one point you switched to English, did you?

Yes, well, this is I think happening now.

Will you tell me about it? It is most interesting that you started writing in one language and then switched.

Yes. I had been writing in Punjabi for the last twelve or thirteen years quite regularly, and I published a book of poetry in 1976 and then a book of short stories in 1982. And so I have been writing in Punjabi basically all the time. But in the last two to three years, I translated some of my poems for some reason, and when I shared those with some people I knew, they really encouraged me.

My problem is that if I write something in English, or translate that, it will probably not make much sense to people because I am coming from a different background. And then I wrote some that were original in English, and they were sort of . . . we'll see. They encouraged me. That's how it began.

Still writing poetry?

Still writing poetry, but at the same time for the last four or five years I have known a theatre group we have. It is basically some friends who work on a volunteer basis, and we get together almost every week now and do some theatre. And for that theatre we wrote some plays in Punjabi and then we wrote them in English. They are not simply literal translations of the Punjabi versions, but we wrote them in English as well, and we produced them in English. Basically my English writing is those plays and poetry. I have not written nor translated any of my short stories into English.

Is that going to come next?

Yes, I think it will. Because I am sort of getting used to the idea now. When I have been invited to read some of my poetry in some functions, the response has been really great. It encourages one to do that, and I have been reading and writing English from grade six. So English is something. I still have this love and hate relationship with the language.

Tell me about it.

Well, it happened when I was in high school in grade six, I would say. The type of education system we have in India, and I think it is still pretty well intact, is that if you don't do well in a subject you get beaten up every day in the class.

By whom?

By the teachers. It may have changed now because I have been away for twenty-two years. I was beaten up almost every day for my English. I didn't know English that well, and even to this day I feel this lack of confidence in the language because I was beaten up by those teachers. The poor fellows, you know, I can tell now they didn't know much themselves. But that is how the system worked. So you know English is something I have been trying to learn all of my life, and at that same time trying to escape from it because I don't like it—I have been beaten up so much because of it.

This is fascinating. I have never heard anything like this.

So you know I do most of my reading in English now. I do read a lot of Punjabi stuff, magazines and books that I get from India, but most of the things that I read now are in English, and a lot of people I know now and communicate with are English. So it is not something that I have had to sort of relearn, to write in English. I think it is simply that I have to make a switch. Now I think I am finding that audience that could read what I am writing. Before, I had no idea that somebody would read what I am writing in English.

The emotional scars you have received from the beatings, do they go deep?

I think that I have sort of overcome that now. But at one time they were deep.

How old are you now?

I am forty-two. For a while, after I came to Canada in 1967, I started my education right from grade 8 again, just because of this whole system we had there. I had no confidence at all that I could do anything, or that I did anything. So what I did was, after work I would take night school courses in English here in Canada. I eventually found a job in the post office which was much lighter work than the mill work, and I had a lot of time on my hands. I kept going to school and eventually did a masters degree at SFU (Simon Fraser University) while working full time.

A masters in what?

Sociology. I think the reason that I did that is because I simply wanted to prove to myself that I could do something. Because of the education back in India, it sort of beat the self-respect of my soul out of me, and I wanted to get that back into me. I think I have probably been a bit successful.

Are you working with sociology?

No. I work as a part-timer in the post office on weekends, and I also have another part-time job helping somebody teach Punjabi at UBC.

So it is sort of nice, easy work that leaves you time to pursue your intellectual interests?

Yes. Sociology, I thought, would have been helpful in all those things, doing theatre or literature, or just understanding things. I haven't regretted that I spent all that time on getting the degree, I am very happy I did.

What are the main influences in your writing? I should say, what are the general subjects of your poems?

Basically about me, but not as an individual. It is about the community that I am a part of. Most of my writings, poetry and short stories, have been about the experiences here as an immigrant and also about going back and forth. When you are sitting at home on weekends and entertaining friends and other people, you always talk about back home. The experiences keep coming back. They are part of the life here. You are never here.

You live here, but you are always making references to what happened there and how you did these things there. You continue to compare things. The picture has been not of myself only. It deals with both worlds: life here and back there. Sometimes you go back and have some sort of experiences and that becomes part of the writing.

So I have been writing about what people feel. I mean the Indo-Canadian people. How I feel, how the people I know in the community feel. Also some of the experiences here, the racism. The plays we did deal with the farm workers. Sometimes you see in Vancouver a lot of older Indo-Canadians sitting at bus stops or in the parks because they really don't have any other place to go. There is no centre for them.

So that becomes a subject we write about, to show it is a kind of social commitment: These people need a place. Sometimes (the subject is) women's suppression in the community, and how women are still oppressed because we have this feudal background. But my poetry also deals with—at least in the beginning it dealt with—the political situation in India. How some people were trying to bring change, and about the recent problems in the Punjab over the last four or five years.

Some of the poems I have written recently deal with that. I have been writing about my own experiences here as well. I have written a number of poems that deal with my work, being a postman. A letter-carrier. Basically I think it is the content of the life I live, and about the other people I know. So that is the content of my writings.

Do you have any anger in you about the racism that you or others have experienced here?

Yes. Very much so.

Will you express it to me in the way a writer looks at it?

I think I have gone through a bit of a change as far as anger is concerned. When I came here, I was simply angry at things. Why was I being looked at as something that is second class, something not equal to other people? But then, going to school, taking sociology and all that, has changed a lot of things. I have become, I guess, a bit more philosophical.

You understand the reasons why people are like that?

Right. I am not as angry as I was before. But it still hurts. Before, when I would go out of the house I would look for signs that this is racism and that is racism. I was so involved in that kind of experience myself that this person is looking at me, and it is racism in his eyes, and in this situation and that situation. Somehow I don't do that any more.

If something hits me, or (somebody) calls me a name, it is very obvious that I would notice it. Otherwise I go around doing my things and just being what I am. That, I think, is a change from my earlier days, when I actually went out and looked for things, and I saw a lot of things that were racist and directed towards me. So, I don't really look for it. I am not that angry any more, but it is part of my existence, racism.

It's there. It's at work. It's with people when I go to a door to deliver a parcel. Sometimes through their window they see only an

East Indian face—I don't have my hat on most of the times, their face says something else. When they open the door and they see me as a postman it is totally different. It changes.

It changes? Suddenly you are accepted then?

Right! Suddenly you see that change. It is so subtle. You can feel it, but it is hard to explain what went on in that moment.

I don't think most of us understand what it is to be on the receiving end of racism. Every book that describes it is different. I would like to read more about this.

Well, let's hope that one day I write something about it. I am not sure that I will, because it is part of my life, and not to make somebody angry, or get even with somebody, but just to express myself. Yes.

Why do you write? Have you made some money with it?

I made fifty dollars last week! And that is the only money I ever made in writing.

But is that important?

No. If it was important, I would not be doing it. No, it is not. But one of the reasons, when I think of writing in English, I think money does somehow enter into that picture. Yes. As far as Punjabi is concerned, everybody already accepts the obvious that there is no money to be made when you write a book and pay from your own pocket to be published. Then, if you have the energy, and you want to do it, you can go around and sell it yourself, otherwise it just sits there. But in English, the chances are that if you write something, you might be able to make some money.

But no, as far as writing is concerned, it is not for money.

Well, there is always the day of the big breakthrough. For instance, I think he is a countryman of yours, Rohinton Mistry.

Yes, I think I have seen a novel by him.

He is suddenly presented to us as an important writer. As is Michael Ondaatje, from Sri Lanka. And other people. So literature in Canada is

going to change through people like you. What do you think of Canadian
literature from what you have read?

I have very mixed feelings about Canadian literature. I try to read
and familiarize myself with the country's writings because I live here.
But most of the time I don't understand, especially poetry. I mean
somehow I don't get any feeling out of it. There are some people
whom I sort of read more, but they are—I don't think they have a
very high standing as far as the literary circles go in Canada. There
are some things I like. There is this fellow, Robin Mathews. I read
some of his poems. This was way back, ten or twelve years ago,
probably, and at that time things were happening in India, sort of
revolutionary, and we were writing that kind of poetry. I understood
and liked what he wrote. At the same time, when I was reading a lot
of other people, I couldn't understand what they were saying. They
were such, I don't know, highly intellectual exercises.

A lot of things you can say about it. But my feeling was, if I can't
get anything out of it, if I have to look in the dictionary at every line,
every five words, to make some sense out of it, I lose interest in that.

You are talking about literature by élitists for élitists.

Most of the literature I have found here, well, my feeling is that it
belongs to that category. But, you know, at a local level, for instance
in Vancouver, there are a lot of people who are doing things at a
local level. Getting all these poetry readings together, getting
together and writing and publishing. That kind of thing I quite
enjoy. But the people who are at the top of things—I haven't been
able to make any link with them.

Well, I suppose this has a lot to do with where we come from. Let's talk about
emotions, Anglo-Saxon Canadian emotions. Keeping emotions to themselves.
You don't get praise from them. You don't get condemnation. They don't
show joy or fear as far as they can help it. The books are different. There, it
seems, the whole hidden world of emotion erupts. How does that compare with
your world? How do you deal with emotions? Do you show them?

I think we are opposite to what you describe about the Anglo-Saxon
here. We are much more emotional, I think, on a personal level.
People show emotions—like if you are reading poetry, the sort of
traditional way of showing praise is that you praise it right there,

"Great! Great!" and all that, even clap sometimes. I think as far as writing is concerned, the effort has been to turn away from that in writing. It is to be more, I don't know if you can say, rational.

More contained?

Yes. Not so obvious in your expressions of your emotions. Contained. I guess that would be the word. But in everyday life, people are quite emotional, and they get angry very fast. In the writing, as I said here, the people are trying to become more professional or businesslike. I don't necessarily like that. I like to see emotions.

When I came in 1958, there was virtually no Canadian literature, not the mainstream that we have now. But I have a hunch that this is going to change through the contributions that you and others are making. How do you see this change? Is this going to benefit Canadian literature?

I think so. I see it as a—I am here and I am part of Canada now. Although it is taking a bit longer for everybody to realize that, and there is still resistance, but I am here now. What I do is Canadian, and whether I do it for myself or for the society, it is Canadian. And with literature being part of life, I think it is—I am writing and other people are writing, and other people are going to write, and it will become a part of the Canadian experience. I don't really see it as going to change.

I believe, as you say, that before 1958 or 1950 there was virtually no Canadian literature. Very little. I think Canadian literature is going to become what Canadian society is, and I am going to make an effort on my part in doing that, whether that is seen as a change from something that was before or something that it is going to be. I wasn't here before, so I can't say what it was like. But now, since I am here, I am going to be part of it, and if that changes it, great.

Last night I saw a film by an immigrant writer who writes very good films and television series, and the characters had thick accents from her home country. They spoke a kind of almost cliché-ridden English. This marred the entire production for me, because somebody with a strong accent would not use a very English-Canadian term. What kind of English do you use when you write?

I think the most Canadian type of English that we speak here every day, like in the plays we did. I think the problem came when we actually produced those plays and we had the actors speaking. We tried to make it not a kind of East Indian English but Canadian English. So we had, in places, some terms that we use in Punjabi, and we used them in English where they fit. But other than that we didn't consciously try to do any kind of language tricks, or anything that would make it more Indian or Canadian.

When I go back to Germany, I find myself, for the first week or two, translating from English into German, and people give me strange looks. This is not the German spoken there. My English is now pretty well advanced and has become my working language. This kind of difficulty, translating from one to the other, is what I had in mind.

I think because we haven't been writing in English that much. I haven't been. So it is basically Punjabi (I write), and you do a sort of translation, as you say.

Ah. You speak in Punjabi still.

Most of the time. Two of us have written all those plays together. So it is basically in Punjabi we are thinking. I think it is part of the problem, our Punjabi here that we speak, it is very mixed now. If not half, I would say a good twenty-five per cent is English. And things are the same way back in Punjab, people speak Punjabi, but they have so many English words in it because of the films and the television medium. When you speak, most of the things you do are very identical in both languages.

So, it is not really a big problem of thinking in one and translating into the other. All of these terms are sort of every-day life terms. We have the same terms in Punjabi now. *TV, car, radio, truck, station,* all these words are Punjabi words as well. So the basic every-day language we use has almost become identical in our minds, somehow. I think that is a helpful thing in a way, somehow. But, for the language, Punjabi especially, it is a very bad thing.

There is a curious debate going on in Canada. It was suggested that we all use what has become the in term, people of colour, people like you. They no longer say black man, or black person, or whatever, it is now people of colour. And so, it was suggested the writers of colour can only write about their own experiences, about their own people, about their own environment, about people with their own skin colour. By the same token, if I went to India and spent six months there, it would not be proper for me to write about an inner-Indian conflict between two people. There are some people for it, some against it. What is your feeling? Should we allow you to write about people like me, or Anglo-Saxon Canadians?

That is a difficult question, in a sense, because when somebody writes something, as you said, in the beginning there are two types of writing. One is people who write about other things, which are not always literary writings. But when I write something, I write from my own experience. That is sort of the beginning point, where things began. If I am writing from my own experience, if I am interacting with somebody who is not of the same colour or the same culture, then I have the right to express what he has been saying or what she has been saying or thinking in interaction with me.

But I personally would have problems, or would not feel very confident, to write in a totally detached form about somebody else's culture because I don't have that kind of inner knowledge about the things there. But I, for myself, would in a way oppose that because historically things have been written about my country and my people by whites, and they are not very accurate.

For example, history and a lot of other things, and social sciences. People need to know. But if I am living here and I am in contact with people of all cultures, then I think I can write about something else. Because I have friends at work and friends at school who are from other cultures. I guess, being a sociologist, I can observe what they are doing and can sort of interpret it in my own way.

But it is very hard to take sides on this. Being an Indian myself, and coming from that background, I do have that feeling against a lot of people who have written about us and have given us this . . . this whole thing we see in the popular media, you know, everybody else is criminal and barbaric in their behavior but not the whites. Yet if you look at things, it is the other way around in most cases. Yet, all these things—blacks are more criminal, and Asians are this and that—are a result of other people writing about us. That is how I see it in any sort of large framework.

But a particular person from another culture could be very sympathetic to what I am or what my community is, and I wouldn't object if somebody wanted to write about it. A lot of people have written very sympathetic things. I think it is a difficult question, and I don't know if I can be excited at this time.

I remember the terrible accident in India four or five years ago, with the chemical plant, and two or three thousand people died. There were very few stories of human interest, very little about the suffering they had undergone. The entire discussion, as I recall it in the media, was about the legal responsibility for the accident. Was this company going to make good their promises and was it going to compensate the victims? Was it going to mess up the environment some more? Union Carbide it was. I believe there is deep-seated xenophobia about people of colour, if you like. That they are somehow not quite with us, not quite worth being looked at. Nothing is on the surface. It is all implied.

Yes, I think a lot of things have become very sophisticated now. I have been involved in the last couple of months in looking at the history of this incident that took place in Vancouver seventy-five years ago, the *Komagata Maru* incident.

Right. There was a play written about that, I believe by Sharon Pollock.

Right. By Sharon Pollock. When you read that history at that time, and you pick up a newspaper, the *Province* or the *Vancouver Sun*, they were both around at that time, the racism is so obvious. You can read a line and get mad at it, and then do whatever you want to. But it is there. Everything bad that it could say and print about the Indians or the Sikhs or the Punjabis, they said that, and they never thought twice about it.

But now, things are very sophisticated. You can read it between the lines, and sometimes, if you have this sociological imagination as they call it in sociology, you can sort of pick it up. Otherwise it is very hard to see it. But it is there. It's in the news, it's in the way they select news. What news they are going to show, what part, and what not. It is there. Just this last weekend we did a play about the women's place in society, three stages, how different socializing takes place between a boy and a girl in a house, and how a working wife is treated and the grandmother. We did it at a conference that was taking place in downtown Vancouver.

The news that came out on CTV! In the beginning they showed

this arranged marriage problem in India, and there was this big function, and the way the whole thing was presented—the message that the conference was trying to give, and what the play was about, it was nowhere. I know what happened there. I know my community and I can make sense of it. But for somebody who doesn't have all that basic knowledge about things, all he is going to take from it, you know, is this: "These Hindus! These Indians!"

Do you know any white Anglo-Saxon Canadians that accept you totally, without reservations?

Yes. Some friends. Yes, I would say yes.

I am not quite sure why you chose not to pursue sociology but stayed in the post office. Does it have something to do with your love-hate relationship with English?

It could be. No. For one thing, I did my masters degree—as I did say in my comment earlier—to try and prove myself. I never really thought of it as a way to get a better job. The post office job I have is part-time now, it gives me pretty good security. It has been, so far. It is changing now, very fast. So after I finished my degree in 1986, I haven't really tried to get a job with it. But now, since last year, last summer, I have been working at UBC with this Punjabi teaching job. That came because I had this degree. So, in a way, I am utilizing it. And I am thinking of probably going into a PhD program and pursuing it further. So, I haven't really used it in order to get a specific job, but it is a part of my life now and it has been very useful.

Andrew
Busza

Andrew Busza was born in 1938 in Cracow, Poland, and spent his childhood in the Middle East. He was educated at St. Joseph's College, Beulah Hill, and University College, London, England. He was a member of the London-based *Kontynenty* group of Polish poets (1958 to 1962), and taught English and history in London grammar schools (1963 to 1965). He immigrated to Canada in 1965, and since then has taught in the English department and the Program in Contemporary Literature at the University of British Columbia, Vancouver.

His poetry has appeared in periodicals in Poland and abroad since 1958, as well as in the following anthologies: *Ryby na piasku* (B. Swiderski, London, 1965), *Opinsaniez pamieci* (Panstwowy Instytut Wydawniczy, Warsaw, 1965), *Neue polnische Lyrik* (Karl Hanser Verlag, Darmstadt, 1965), *Nach der Sintflut: eine Auslese neuer polnischer Lyrik* (Munich, 1968), *Contemporary Poetry of British Columbia* (Sono Nis, Vancouver, 1970), *Volvox: Poetry from the Unofficial Languages of Canada in English Translation* (Sono Nis, Vancouver, 1971), *Seven Polish Canadian Poets* (Toronto, 1984), *Znaki wodne* (Instytut Literacky, Paris, 1969), *Astrologer in the Underground* (translated from the Polish by Jagna Boraks and Michael Bullock, Ohio University Press, Athens, Ohio, 1971), *Kohelet* (a long poem published in *Kultura,*

Paris, 1975). He has published two books of poetry translated from Polish with Bogdan Czaykowski: *The Revolution of Things: Selected Poems of Miron Bialoszewski* (Charioteer Press, Washington, 1974), *Gathering Time: Five Modern Polish Elegies* (Barbarian Press, Vancouver, 1984), and is the author of *Conrad's Polish Literary Background* (Institutum Historiscum Polonicum, Rome and London, 1966). He is currently working with J.H. Stape on an edition of Joseph Conrad's *The Rover* (to be published by Oxford University Press).

JURGEN HESSE: Would you tell me something about your background, and how you came to Canada?

ANDREW BUSZA: The Polish version of my first name is Andrzej, Andreas in German. I was born in the south-east of what was Poland, between the wars. Right at the very corner between Rumania and Russia. My grandfather, who was a doctor, had a sanatorium. It was an interesting sort of institution. A sort of combination sanatorium with a spa where people would usually come to spend their summer vacation to bring up their health but also for cultural reasons as well. The sort of thing that nowadays is just taken for granted. He had a policy: If there were twenty free places for artists and writers who— in return for giving talks, giving a performance, playing, or something like that—could stay there several weeks, and they in turn provided the milieu for the people who came. So, when the war broke out—I was only nine months old—we weren't particularly concerned with the German advance because it was far away, but we were very close to the Russian border, and when the Russians crossed the border on the 17th of September, 1939, there was an English military mission in the area under a general which was investigating the diplomatic climate. They in fact knew my parents because we had English visitors before the war, and they came to my uncle and my father and said, "Look, the Russians are going to be here within two hours. We are moving over to Rumania, and we suggest that you do the same." And so, that is just what we did.

Otherwise you would probably not be here.

I would not be here. My brother was born there. Then, as German pressure increased we, with the help of some English Quakers, moved to Cyprus. You remember, Crete was taken by German paratroopers. There was a similar kind of fear that the same would happen to Cyprus. So, again, we moved through Turkey to Palestine. Palestine at that time was a British mandate. My childhood was essentially (in) Palestine. First living in Tel Aviv and then a place on the way to Jerusalem, and then Jerusalem. So, I first actually went to school there.

And your English?

I didn't know any English at that point. I moved in a sort of a Polish bubble, if you like. With my mother, grandparents. My father in the meantime had gone off and joined the Allied Forces. He was a doctor, and he found his way up to Scotland. I really grew up in a—linguistically speaking—very complicated context because for instance, to start with, we lived in a Jewish area, Jewish home. Then we move to an Arab (area). When we went to a shop, a Jewish shop, very often my mother would speak German. If we went to Arab shops, she spoke French. Then there was English. I went to a Polish school which was in the Greek colony next to the German colony in Jerusalem. That's my childhood. The Mediterranean of which I am still very fond.

And then I came to England. Towards the end of 1947 it became evident there was going to be serious trouble. In some ways I was lucky. I missed the war because I was away from it. My only experience with the war was (in) 1943 when we had the Allied armies conducting major manoeuvres in the Middle East in preparation for the invasion of Italy.

I remember once a single German plane in Tel Aviv dropping a bomb. I remember going down to a shelter—this was probably during the North African campaign—but that is about it. For me the real war experience came in 1946, during the terrorist campaign of the *Irgun Zwai Leumi.* Then (the former Israeli prime minister Menachem) Begin was trying to get rid of the English. That is my war in a sense. I almost got blown up with the King David Hotel, actually. In August of 1946.

You were then a lad of eight. A very impressionable age.

Absolutely. Yes. As it became clear that there was going to be trouble we—actually my father was in England and helped to organize this—we made our way to England. I arrived in England in November of 1947 without knowing any English. Then I was put into an English boarding school, in London, and gradually acquired English. I still remember going to a school—my first school in London and going into a classroom. There was a lesson in mathematics, and they were doing long division, and I did not understand a single word of what was being spoken. Then, interestingly enough, I don't remember the actual process of acquiring English. It seems, I suppose, I have repressed it, but it came. I suddenly found myself speaking the language. I do recall having problems with writing and, for instance at the very beginning, instead of playing football on Wednesday afternoons, I was supposed to do English spelling, which actually I didn't mind because I didn't like football. After that, gradually my English improved, and then I eventually went to university in London.

But in the meantime, when I was about fourteen years old, I started writing poetry, and interestingly enough I started writing in Polish in the English boarding school. I felt in many respects isolated and alienated at school, so I think this probably contributed to the fact that I used a language different from the language in which I was operating. Mind you, I was spending my holidays and the occasional weekend at home where Polish was spoken. So I continued to live essentially in two worlds. The school world was English. Even some of my pleasure reading was in Polish, so I sort of moved in between two languages. I have been a schizophrenic all my life.

I wasn't going to mention that.

Yes, I continued to be a schizophrenic. And of course, as you know, being bilingual entails not only the question of the language which we use, but also our attitudes. I would even suggest our emotions. Our emotions are probably a little bit different when one is operating in one linguistic context and then another one. When I am speaking to Poles, and then when I am speaking to Englishmen and Canadians, I am a slightly different person, I think.

In Canada I tend to tone down my gesticulation because people are so afraid, they stonewall you if you become too emotional.

It is really uncanny the way in which one's attitudes are affected by this phenomenon. Now, furthermore this can also acquire a sort of perverse dimension. I have on occasions found that in an English environment—in order to impress my audience with my exoticism—I will play up my Polishness. I have visited Poland on a number of occasions, and there have been occasions when I have been deliberately more English, more Anglo-Saxon in my attitudes. So it is complicated.

When I go to Germany I always make sure that they know I am no longer a German but a Canadian. But they don't care. My German is still word-perfect. The perversity of that is interesting. Why do you think we do this?

Is it bragging? I think defence has something to do with it. But I think even with Polish, one of the things that I have found over the years is that my attitude towards Polishness has changed. It is not something static, and I suppose it has something to do with age, but external factors contribute as well. I have found that since the late seventies and eighties dramatic changes have taken place in Poland, with Solidarity and so on. In fact a new generation has taken over. The Polish society has changed character. You must remember that I was brought up in a time capsule. I was brought up in a Polish emigré environment among people who were brought up themselves in the inter-war period. So, I still have this common language with people who in a sense were brought up in a comparable environment, who belong to that world.

Through these recent dramatic changes which have taken place in Poland that world has been gradually eroding and disappearing. In other words, the new generation which has now arrived on the scene do not have exactly the same set of values, the same attitudes, similar experiences. These are people who no longer remember the pre-war period.

And they don't care. In many respects they actually irritate me. So that is the point at which I adopt my British mask, my English mask. Of course, as in your case you mentioned Italy, my life is also complicated because I am Polish, I am British, and I am sort of a Canadian. There is this certain hierarchy of emotional authenticity. I think I can say that at the emotional level I am most Polish. Then comes 'Englishness'; in many ways I am more English than Canadian.

You mean the élitism, the literary workings?

I am afraid so. Yes. And then, my Canadian consciousness which is the latest and perhaps most superficial. Now, I have been here a long time, since 1965. I was already a formed person when I came here, and I go back to England frequently.

JH:Do we change? Do we adapt fully to the Canadian lifestyle?

I have found it very difficult. There is another schizophrenia that operates, of course, and that is the schizophrenia of being an academic working in the university environment. In another bubble. Disconnected from reality. In the university I feel, in many ways, a sort of a schizophrenic. I perform my university duties. I love literature, but I am very much at odds with the university as an institution and with the direction it has been moving, generally. It is a world that increasingly irritates me. It is moving in a direction that is anathema to me.

In my writing, I use other languages than English. I use French, Italian, Latin, German. That is how my writing is coloured. It is what occurs at the time. People think that I am grandstanding.

It is natural for us.

In Europe if you are a multinational, multilingual intellectual, you use everything that comes to your mind. The same happens in Mexico, in intellectual circles. Does this kind of multicultural experience—the hardship which befell most of the people I have interviewed who have been through the war—influence our writing? We've suffered creatively. Is it true that creative suffering, when you deal with it on an intellectual positive level rather than becoming a professional victim as so many people do, does that make us interesting writers with more to say than a Canadian like W.O. Mitchell, or Margaret Atwood?

Atwood. Whose work I dislike for that very reason. You know it is the self-pity. It is the professional victim aspect that really irritates me.

In general, the writings of the immigrant writers are not well-known by the

*general public. Most of the immigrant writers I have interviewed don't seem
to write blockbusters, thrillers, escapist literature. Why is this?*

I don't know. (Mr. Busza pauses, uninterested in the question.)

I mentioned that I started writing poetry in school, in Polish,
and at that point I was actually beginning to lose my Polish. So, when
I was writing Polish I was actually already having problems with the
language. My Polish improved when I went to university. I was at the
university in London, and although I was attending lectures and
studying, I in fact spent most of my free time with a rather interesting milieu of slightly older young people than myself who were in a
comparable situation. Poles in London. We would meet in cafés,
pubs, all of us had literary ambitions of one kind or another. We
started editing a literary monthly, and this group was really active for
about ten years. At that point I was writing poetry in Polish. In effect,
as the group grew up, people went in different directions. One of
them returned to Poland. He has since then been a translator of
Shakespeare, working in the theatre. Actually three of us are in
Canada, one is in London. Another one is a colleague of mine here
at the university, Bogdan Czaykowski, who is a very good poet. Some
stayed in England, but it was a group of people who were writing,
although all of us were able to write in English—we all knew English
very well. Nevertheless we continued writing in Polish. Our work was
published both in England and Poland as well, translated. I have two
of my poems translated into German.

Can you write as well in English as in Polish?

What has happened was that in the late seventies I came to a sort of
impasse. I was writing less, and I then decided to shift into English.
I have been writing poetry in English since that time, but I have been
very reluctant not only to publish it, but even to show it to anyone.
There is a very strong resistance. I suppose it is a fear that I will not
be understood. But the reason that I decided to make this move was
because of teaching English at the university, working constantly in
English. I have come to realize that in effect I know that language
technically speaking much better. I am now moving into prose, and
I hope that this might be my solution.

I have sort of, as it were, made my academic career with Conrad.
I published a monograph on his Polish background, and it has

become a sort of an important position. I suppose the reason why I have been able to write on him, and I have been interested in him, is because of some of the parallel experiences. Now, Conrad's case is an interesting one. Here we have a young man who learns a language at the age of twenty-one, which is even later than myself, and who is able to use that language creatively. How do we account for that? Very difficult. But I have a theory which runs as follows. You see, in order to use language creatively the way a poet uses language, in a sense what is crucial are the early years, in childhood. The moment when words are connected to things for the first time. When you name a flower for the first time. When you say 'rose' when you are describing that flower. When you first name emotions. That is the crucial moment. You know, even to this day I would argue— and probably your experience is the same—the word 'rouge' is somehow emotionally more authentic for me than the word 'rose' in English.

There are many words that are more authentic. In other words, one could argue that unless someone is born into the language that, in a sense, it is almost impossible to write, as a poet, in another language. I think (this is) because you discovered the world for the first time in that language. Now I think Conrad's case was interesting. What he wrote about to start with anyway, were experiences which he first had in English, as a sailor. You see, he did not have a Polish vocabulary for that world. He made a dramatic move (to) a completely new environment, from a landlocked experience to the sea experience, and to life in exotic parts of the world, like Malaysia, like Africa. These were experiences which he first, as it were, to a degree had in the English language, and so some of the connections between words and things took place in his mind already in English.

What about Conrad's syntax. Is that the syntax of an English writer?

Not quite. There is a difference. In the area of syntax you can detect certain foreignness. It is a combination of French and Polish, because he learned French first, and he in fact spoke French throughout his life more fluently than English. He spoke French with an *accent du midi*, whereas when he spoke English, he always spoke English with a strong foreign accent which interestingly enough deteriorated and became more obvious as he grew old.

When I write, I write in a completely Anglo-Saxon syntax. It is a 'thing' language. It describes other people's events, and I stick with facts. When I write fiction, I find that my sentences do not want to end. I write Hemingway sentences, sometimes a whole page long. Readers here aren't used to this style. It is very German, written in English. So a good friend made the suggestion, why don't you translate it yourself into German, or rewrite it in German?

Yes, I understand this perfectly.

The thought patterns cannot be erased. In what language do you think now?

It depends. I have just written a piece called *My Great Grand Uncle's Bequest*, which will appear in the next issue of *Canadian Literature*, and which is in fact a sort of ideal there with a great great uncle of mine, a sort of personality in an Eastern European context. I have introduced a certain amount of stylization, drawing upon Polish writing. So, the subject matter is Polish, but the style, well, I am very curious as to how the Anglo-Saxons are going to respond to this. My hope is that they will find it exotic and hence interesting.

Let me go into an area such as your position at the university, that of an essayist, of a literary thinker and critic. What about Canadian literature? Have immigrant writers influenced Canadian literature at all?

I really don't know. I really don't know. The thing is this. I suppose I am in a slightly more fortunate position than you are in this respect, because in the university environment—in the English department in which I teach and where I am also involved in the comparative literature program—I have an opportunity to teach French, German, and Polish authors on occasion. Now, in that environment one is actually in a multicultural—from a literary point of view a more cosmopolitan—environment. We have specialists who deal with Canadian literature. I am not involved in that. So my reading of Canadian literature is limited. There are certain authors' works which I enjoy. Or, for example, I was recently reading poems with my students, say by Earle Birney, and there are Canadian writers whom I find interesting and intriguing. But, I suppose essentially as a reader of literature I really don't limit myself to one national literature. I know English literature probably best, but I also read French literature, I read German literature, I read even Latin, which is still alive for me. I read Spanish, Latin American literature. Now, where was I going to go from there?

Canadian literature, have we influenced it?

Interestingly enough, I know for example that literature in England, British literature, has been influenced. There are a number of British poets now who acknowledge the influence, for instance, of East European writing. They are interested in it. One of my projects for this summer, I will be doing two things. I will be writing an introduction to a Conrad novel. His last completed novel, which he wrote at your age (65). It is set in the South of France and is about a man who was a pirate all his life and who returns to France, back to his home in order to retire. He wants to go back to his roots. He happens to arrive during the Revolution, and so life is complicated. This was the first Conrad book that I read when I was still at school, when I was fourteen. And I remember vividly really enjoying this book, while my fellow pupils did not like it at all. I was really puzzled by this. Anyway, that is one thing.

My other project, I will be writing about these sort of problems, the problem of writing in an alien environment, exile, and so on, and that is going into a volume of essays on modern Polish poetry, which is being published in England by a Welsh Publisher. Now obviously there is interest in the subject matter. So, I have noticed since around the mid-fifties, I think, there has been an interest in Eastern European writing. It is probably connected with the Common Market. England has opened up and culturally has certainly become much more open.

What about the obverse of the question? Have we been influenced by the Canadian experience in our writing?

Oh yes, there is no question about it. For example, my best friend here, Bogdan Czaykowski, whom I have known since 1957 and who was part of that group. If you read his poetry you will find how the Canadian landscape is a very major concern of his. He writes very beautifully about the Okanagan, for example.

Landscape or people?

Landscape. Not people. That is a very good point. There are no people. He is not like Robert Frost. It is landscape.

Yes, the immense landscape that cannot be duplicated because it is unique to this country.

Now, one of the problems which I have encountered here, which I didn't have in England—you see in England I did have a milieu. Here, I have found it impossible to find a milieu.

Describe what a milieu is.

A group of people who are related to one another, not professionally. That is crucial. But through their intellectual artistic passions. I suppose that really is the crucial factor because they may disagree in many ways. Now, we formed this milieu in London. We were a very diverse group, but we could meet in a café and talk for hours about things which concerned us. I stress the fact that this is not a professional connection. Our group consisted of people—there was an historian, someone who had worked in films, poets—a variety. In fact some of us were teachers, some were working in journalism, many of us were students, but we formed a milieu. Now, I have not been able to find such a milieu here. I have not been able to find a common language with the Vancouver writers. They write about a world that is completely alien to my world. My milieu are the books, I suppose. Now there is one group of people with whom I do occasionally have a real contact—my students.

Right. I know of three groups I have met throughout the years. The first one was around George Bowering, when he held court at the Cecil Hotel. He was the grand master of language, and people came to adore him. This was in the hippie times. The second was very similar, but in a different direction. Raymond Hull, who was the co-author of The Peter Principle, *and a very down-to-earth nonfiction writer. He is dead now. He collected people around him in soirées, to pick their brain for future book ideas. Neither group was very substantial. But then there is the group around Karl Sandor. A daring poet. He is published in British and Canadian literature magazines. Very powerful. They meet every Thursday evening and wage gigantic verbal battles. They are not all writers. This group has kept on going for years, but it is almost to the exclusion of anyone that I know. I don't go there very much because usually my life takes me to other places. But I agree, the draw is not to this kind of thing.*

Interesting. Well I think one of the problems here is the professionalization of life. Writing has become a professional activity.

Could we say business?

Yes, business. That is what I mean. Exactly. People write to make money. You acquire a reputation when your book makes money.

Let's take an example: Bill Deverell, a thriller writer. He won a $50,000 prize for his first book. I believe he considers himself to be part of Canadian literature, and who I am to say he isn't? He has a large presence and a high profile. Yet the poets who abound are not recognized.

There are lots of them! The other problem here—and this is actually a particularly Canadian problem more so than in the States—is the fact that intellectual life seems to me to a significant degree to be focussed on the university. It is almost the case that, in a sense, you don't have intellectuals who are not in some way related or connected to the university. Now, I think this is an impoverishing phenomenon. Because the university has its own ideology. The university is a very peculiar institution, which has in fact evolved in a direction which is increasingly inimical to creative work. It has become much more bureaucratized. It moves towards greater conformism in thought. It is being affected by the mechanisms of mass society.

    You see, just as the media are affected by the mechanisms of mass culture, the same phenomenon is taking place at the university as well. We have certain fads, for example, in methodology. And unless you follow this fad, you are going to be discriminated against. You are not going to succeed. Now that I think is a very dangerous environment for a writer.

It leads, I think, into a sort of linguistic desert. Let's talk about the importance of language, which is the only tool we have. Can you philosophize about this?

Well, I think there are a number of factors involved. The most obvious factor is of course the importance of the visual media in our time. Television, film, etc. The younger generation reads much less than we used to. There is no question about that. That is an obvious thing. But I think we have another factor. Because this is a multi-ethnic, multilingual community society, there has developed a kind of English, a *lingua franca*. An English which is poorer in expression, in syntax, in diction. If you have got a Canadian of Polish origin speaking to a Canadian of Greek origin, they will use a simpler English to communicate. What I think is lacking here is a demotic Canadian. There is no demotic Canadian.

We don't have that as they have it in Greek. Katharevousa, *the language of scholars, and* demotiki, *the language of the people. Wonderful.*

Yes. With idioms. With original metaphors and so on. From where do the young people draw these metaphors, these expressions? They take them from the media. From the hack writers. From Hollywood. From the stereotype, the clichés.

All the thriller literature is like that, including John Le Carré who is much feted.

To take another example of a wooden writer is in fact my compatriot Jerszy Kosinski. I don't like his work. I think he writes a wooden English. In fact I think he has learned that English primarily from the media. It is *Time Magazine* writing. So I think one of the problems is that, because I am living in the university, I don't have contact with people who speak a language that comes out of the soil, as it were.

We are undergoing change here in Canada, a shift in immigration from predominantly European to predominantly Third-World countries. These people whom I have interviewed are all poets, writing primarily in Punjabi and Italian and Polish, and other languages. The general public, if there is such a thing, never hears about it. Can you look at this a little bit? What is that going to do to writing?

I think particularly the sect of the immigrants from the Orient. They are going to be really the—that is a particularly interesting question mark. Because we are dealing here with a completely different culture. Now this could lead to something very interesting, actually. Already someone like Salman Rushdie suggests the possibilities. Very interesting possibilities. Unfortunately I know very little about these things.

Poles in North America are a slightly different phenomenon say to Germans. Because the Poles who came to America, the original immigrants, were in fact very much the underprivileged. This was an economic immigration. These were peasants. People who could not make it in Europe, and they for a long time were the very bottom of Canadian-North American society.

Like the Third-World people who are coming in today.

Exactly. They had a very strong sense of inferiority vis-a-vis the Canadian society, the Anglo-Saxon establishment. Now my situation is different, of course, because I have come from Europe, with both a European and more specifically Polish past which gives me a sense of cultural, intellectual identification, and where I do not need to feel inferior in any sense. So there is a very important difference.

We are all, I think, prone to these kind of influences. You came secure in the knowledge that you had London University in your background.

Yes, as well as my Polish background. For example, my uncle was a doctor and a writer. He died last year. So, (I have) an interesting and rich background that I can fall back on whenever my identity is in any sense threatened. I mean, I can talk to Margaret Atwood without feeling inferior. Because I have got something even more superior behind me. The other issue that we haven't talked about at all is the question of an audience.

We talked earlier about a milieu. When you have a milieu the milieu to some extent provides you with a kind of virtual reader and you write for this milieu.

Yes, you imagine a generic reader.

That's right. Now when I moved to Vancouver I lost that milieu. Yes, there is a readership in Poland but as time goes on it becomes increasingly blurred. So I am faced with the problem of finding another reader, an imagined reader. And, because I am there at the university in this bubble, amongst people who are interested in creative writing only in a parasitic way—most of them don't seem to be interested in writing, it is something to be processed—now, I don't want to write for people like that. So, I look for an audience. I have very little contact because I am so busy at working. Very little contact on a more casual, natural, personal level with ordinary

Canadians who, in any case, don't read. It is a problem. The reader is something of an abstraction.

There must be people out there who, like (University of British Columbia English Professor) Ron Hatch, are open, generous, interested in widening the scope of their experience.

Let's tie all of this into a bundle. The audience, I think, is the biggest concern of the writer, next to finding a publisher. Can we create an audience?

The writers who really remain are the ones who succeed in doing this. We have had writers in the past who—like (Franz) Kafka—needed an audience. It took him time. Gradually he created an audience for himself. One has to be patient. I am very patient. I have no other way.

Is there anything wrong with becoming known posthumously?

No, why not? And then if what one does is not worthwhile, it will go, it will go. If it is worthwhile, it will last longer than the bestsellers. If we go back into history, bestsellers are often flashes in the pan.

Jan Drabek

Jan Drabek was born in Prague, Czechoslovakia, in 1935. He escaped to West Germany in 1948, and later that year immigrated to the United States. He came to Canada in 1965, and settled in Vancouver. He received his B.A. in English Literature at the American University, Washington, D.C., and also studied at the University of Mysore, India; University of British Columbia; and Simon Fraser University. Mr. Drabek is a former president of the Federation of British Columbia Writers and a former chairman of the B.C. Caucus of The Writers Union of Canada. He is a former vice-president of the Czechoslovak Association of Canada.

His publications include *Blackboard Odyssey* (J.J. Douglas, Vancouver, 1973), personal observations from various European classrooms; *Whatever Happened to Wenceslas?* (Peter Martin Associates in English, 68 Publishers in Czech, both Toronto, 1975), a novel about an immigrant boy in the U.S. and Canada; *Melvin the Weather Moose* (Holt, Rinehart & Winston, Toronto, 1976), a children's story about a moose who could predict weather; *Report on the Death of Rosenkavalier* (McClelland and Stewart in English, 68 Publishers in Czech, both Toronto, 1977), a novel; *The Lister Legacy* (General, Toronto, 1980; also Beaufort Publishing in New York, and Paper Jacks in Canada, 1982), a World War II thriller; *The Statement* (General, Toronto,

1982), a novel about a revolution on a mythical South Pacific island; and *The Golden Revolution* (Macmillan of Canada, Toronto, 1989), a nonfiction book about the new generation of retirees.

Short stories and articles by Mr. Drabek have appeared in *The Malahat Review, The Canadian, Ethos, Reader's Digest, The Globe and Mail,* and others. *Father's Return to Auschwitz,* a documentary film which Mr. Drabek wrote and produced in 1985, is used in Holocaust studies across Canada. He has translated into English a number of plays and essays by Czech authors. His translation of Zdena Skvorecky's novel, *Ashes, Ashes, All Fall Down,* was published by 68 Publishers in Toronto in 1987.

JURGEN HESSE: Would you tell me a little bit about your background, and how you came to be in Canada?

JAN DRABEK: In 1948 when the Communists took over Czechoslovakia my father did not want to stay there anymore, and so we skied out into Bavaria. We escaped on skis and spent three months in Germany, three months in France. I was twelve. While in Germany I celebrated my thirteenth birthday. By September of the same year we were in the United States, in New York. We lived in New York from 1948 until 1954. In 1953, however, I went off to university in Virginia and flunked out of that university in 1957. I went into the U.S. Navy, spent two years in the Navy and came back to get my degree in Washington. I then went off to Europe for two years, to India for a year where I met a Canadian girl whom I eventually married, and moved with her to Vancouver. Here we have lived happily ever after.

How do you rate your ethnic influence on your writing?

Well, where do you draw the line on ethnic? It is of course partially ethnic, but the fact that my father and the family went through such wild adventurous times during and after the war, this practically forced me into writing. I feel that there was an awful lot of story to be told there. Obviously it would not have happened if we had lived in the U.S. It wasn't the ethnicity as such, but the wild juxtaposition of the different things that happened to me that forced me into becoming a story-teller eventually. I fought it for a long time, but then I lost.

Why would you fight it?

Because I had other things to do. I didn't really start writing until I was thirty. Oh, I wrote short stories and newspaper articles and reports and things like that, but up until then I was too busy checking out new places to be really tied down anywhere. And the one place I had been, where it had been suggested that I should become a professional writer, i.e. for the *Washington Evening Star*. I quickly left there when I realized that it was going to cramp my style, that I would have to stay in Washington to sort of go through the lower echelons of being a newspaperman, and I just did not want to do that. I felt I was being too tied down by it all.

Can you compare what you write now with anything that a Canadian-born writer would put out? I am not talking about style and content, but the way you write.

Obviously I have an incredible amount of reservoir because of the things that happened to the family very early while I was still a kid, and the big, incredible changes in the family situation. From being on the top of the heap to being absolutely the lowest, and then sneaking out of the country. All of these things were moving me into a situation where I wanted to put it down on paper. I don't see how something like that could have happened had I lived in a small town in Saskatchewan or anywhere in North America. That would have been rather difficult to come up with. That is why, perhaps unfairly, I sometimes become impatient with too much examination of the small town in Saskatchewan. It is a difficult thing. I admit that if I had been brought up there, and if the initial influences had been by that small town, that I would have had a tough time getting away from it, but it is not the centre of the universe, and my books are not even centred in Prague, which would be pretty much the centre of Europe. They move all around. They move from Czechoslovakia to Germany to Austria, to finally . . . my last novel in 1982 was *The Statement*, which took place in an island in the South Pacific. I needed a completely new place that had not been discovered by anybody else in order to tell my story that I wanted to tell, and so I was able to transfer a lot of the things that I had seen elsewhere in the world to this little island.

It is much more complicated in my case than just simply, here I was born in Prague and here I am living in Vancouver now. Here you have those two poles, and they sort of pull. There was an awful lot of little pulleys which are pulling me in different directions as well, and that is why it is so difficult to answer and say, this is Europe and this is North America. There is an awful lot in between.

You said that you get impatient about, for instance, the description of a small town life in Saskatchewan. However, one must be lenient with Canadian-born writers because unless they are Mordecai Richler who has a famous street in Montreal as a background, they really don't have anything much to write about.

What you are saying, 'lenient' in other words is, perhaps, I am also jealous of them in a sense, because in certain ways they do have an advantage of having had a calm youth which in certain cases can strengthen the reflective abilities and does not make them move in ten different directions. So, I am just saying that it would be difficult for me as I see it now, but it is possible to write about it. Maybe when I say that, I would be unable to do it, and that I become impatient, maybe there is a little bit of jealousy speaking out of that too. Perhaps I would like to be there. To have an awful lot of disappointments and the tragedies that were part of the family life in the Old Country because it was not a small town in Saskatchewan . . . I would have traded them for the calm and, perhaps periodically, a slightly boring experience.

But let's get back to the Canadian who was born on the Prairies. I would assume that having looked at—or having read his stuff— authors coming from the outside of that Saskatchewan town, that this writer would be enticed to get the hell out of there and start seeing things a little bit. And I don't mean taking the three-week tour of Belgium type of thing. I mean really going to live abroad for months, perhaps years at a time, so that the things that he or she writes later on will reflect this comparison. Because we are aware the world is shrinking, and while it might have been O.K. in the thirties and maybe in the twenties to be writing about the small town in Saskatchewan, there is less of a market for it today.

What about Jack Hodgins from Nanaimo who writes about a very, very small world?

He has got a bit of a small world, but he goes to Ireland for his comparisons, and one of his most effective ones, I think it was his second one that had this change and comparison and sort of mysticism between the two. I am talking specifically about the W.O. Mitchells. They are the ones who would probably have trouble today if they were starting with that kind of orientation. In other words, they have become classics for the twenties and thirties, and rightly so, but we are advancing a little bit now. Let us not knock a little town in Saskatchewan. It is just that it is so nicely compact, and you can use it as a symbol, but that same thing would go for a little town in Northern Ontario, or a coast in Nova Scotia. If you reduce your site to that and you start examining it too much, eventually you are going to run out of relevancy, I would say.

Would it be fair to ask who your favourite writers are?

Well, that would be unfair because I was brought into print by Josef Skvorecky. It happened because I wrote to him and said that his *Cowards* I had read in Europe in, I think, the early 1960s. I was so much impressed by this (novel) and thought, oh, wouldn't it be great to have this translated? He wrote back and said, "Look, it's translated already, but since you say you are interested in writing, have you written anything? We are starting a new exile publishing house." Well, I had only an English novel, *Whatever Happened to Wenceslas?* so I sent it to him, and he not only had it translated and published in Czech at 68 Publishers in Toronto, but found an English publisher, Peter Martin Associates, which came out with it in English. So, yes, I have always been a great admirer of Josef Skvorecky, and to me he is topnotch. For example, I think he is head and shoulders above Milan Kundera. I think that Kundera is a yuppie type. I think there is something behind there, there must be something behind there because he sounds an intellectual type of a writer.

Where did you meet Skvorecky?

In Paris. I consider *The Engineer of Human Souls* to be really a topnotch work. Because I am fascinated by structures of novels, and there are few that are as finely structured as that one.

Is there any sense in bracketing out immigrant writers as a special group? Are they significantly different in their writings from the Canadian-born writers? And if they are, in what areas?

You have to approach each one of them on an individual basis. For example, I arrived when I was twelve years old on the shores of this continent. There are some who arrived perhaps earlier. I think (Peter) Newman arrived when he was six or seven. So, there really isn't that much of a difference, and yet he came, and you find very little of his material being influenced, at least I find it so, in Europe. There is perhaps the milieu in which he grew up. The family, European friends and so on influenced him. There are maybe three years difference, and yet because of the involvement of my family, Europe remained very strong for quite a few years even after we left there. My father worked for the *Voice of America* in the (United) States, and so every day he would come home with ethnic press (clippings) from Czechoslovakia, so that I could follow—in *Rude Prado*, which is the Communist Party organ—what was happening over there.

I think that that is what makes the difference. Not necessarily how old you were when you came over, but how much have you maintained? What was your personal attitude in this? There are people who escape from great unpleasantness and economic hardships over there. Economic hardship was not a problem for my family. We came because of human rights. Because of political difficulties that arose over there with the Communists. So, since we left shortly after the Communists took over, there was no revulsion against the Czech scene, which you find among a lot of people who came after 1968 who don't want to have anything to do with Czechoslovakia anymore. They learn English. They plunge into the English-speaking world, and they do everything possible to cut the ties with Europe. They go out of their way to do this. So this is why you have to pick out an individual person and see how the person has been influenced. So if you are looking for a measurement, I don't think you will find any.

It is significant that you didn't change your name, including your first name, and Peter Neumann did change it because he wanted to Anglicize himself. He also went to Upper Canada College as far as I know, which would tend to eradicate ethnic ties. How many of the 1968 Czech writers whom you know have totally embraced . . .

Again, you are touching on another area and another aspect of the whole thing. It depends on the country as well. For example, Russians, from what I have seen of them, are highly nationalistic, and even though they come into this country, or onto this continent, they sort of bring with them the background, you know, Alexandr Solzhenitsyn (living) in a Vermont domain over there. He really has a Little Russia around him. The Russia he would want it to be. He lives in a sort of a vacuum and criticizes America very strongly—which is fine. Nobody is denying him that right, but I am just pointing out that it is also different by nationalities. I have noticed that a lot of Hungarians have a great pride in the survival of this very small number of people who are sort of an anomaly in the central part of Europe. Plus, when you are talking about Communist Europe, because of the countries today, various approaches so far, various differing regimes. For example, the Hungarian regime has for years been a lot more liberal than the Czech regime.

As a result, contact with the country—the writers from North America can go more easily and return from Hungary. Skvorecky and Kundera, the most important two probably, are very definitely on the shit list in Czechoslovakia. They cannot return.

Even today?

Even today. And if they are mentioned, they are mentioned specifically today as the last regime that is holding in Europe in that sort of neo-Stalinist mode. So the contact has been lost in one sense in that they can't go back, but on the other hand all of the literati that come out of Czechoslovakia will always beat a path to Paris to Kundera's door, or to Skvorecky's door in Toronto. It is a routine thing that you have to go and visit these two who will become world-renowned, and so they do have a contact in another way because people do come and visit them.

Stefan Zweig and Franz Kafka, Kurt Tucholsky, Fritz Lang, Josef von Sternberg, Max Horkheimer, Theodor Wiesengrund Adorno, Bertolt Brecht—many of these writers and film directors immigrated to the United States or to Argentina, or to Sweden, as the case was, and nothing more was heard from them. They ceased to function as creative people. None of them had achieved anything at all in exile. Some committed suicide within a few years, and the others, such as Brecht, couldn't wait to get back quickly enough to Germany. Whereas others, the filmmakers Lang and von Sternberg, produced only trash. So, this is an ethnic displacement.

Well, I wonder how correct you actually are. Bertolt Brecht, after he came back from exile, you could consider him . . . where is Brecht's exile? He was in East Berlin after the war, and he was quite successful there, wasn't he? Franz Werfel's *The Song of Bernadette* was written in exile wasn't it? I think we are dealing again with individuals and how they can take it, and how they cannot take it. Some of my father's friends who were not writers said, "We are going to die here, we are going to stay here, even though it may kill us, because going into exile would be absolute death for us." So they did stay and usually they died, some of them in prison. So that goes for non-writers as well as for writers, and there are some writers who simply could not function elsewhere. There are others who could.

Vaclav Havel.

Vaclav Havel is an interesting type. He was in 1968 in America. I remember my father writing about him because his father and mine were good buddies from good old Prague. Vaclav Havel was at that time instrumental in bringing in the whole idea of re-establishing emigré contacts in Czechoslovakia with the rest of the world, and he was saying how much talent there is among the emigrés, and how much good will, if they could harness it. I think he himself has little by little been pushed, and this comes through in *The Temptation*, the latest one, the Faustian play, where he is trying to deal with this business. How he was pushed into a position of a symbol, and how difficult it is for him to deal with this, and of course that also makes it difficult for him to say, "To hell with this, I am going to go and have a nice time living in New York on my royalties."

There was a race in Vaclav Havel's case, as to whether he was going to become a symbol, or whether he was going to become an exile. He already realized he was a symbol, and if he had left, there would have been nobody.

He became a martyr.

Well, he was a martyr perhaps even before that. He was in prison. It is, again, extremely complicated. It is an individual thing, and the Czech emigré exile press—which is sometimes quite high in quality—is dealing with this: 'Should we leave. Who is right? The person who leaves or the person who stays there and is sort of beaten to death by the rather deadly weight of the regime upon their shoulders.' That is what everybody has to decide. Again, there is no standard measure of the thing.

You know, you mentioned the German (emigré writers), how about Billy Wilder? There is a guy who did fabulously well. You have musicians, even Russians, Swiatoslav Richter and people like that. Mstislav Rostropovich. There are people who just say, 'We are going to do our best,' and they are absolutely making everybody blink. We are watching them wide-eyed as they grow in stature in the west.

I hope I'm correct in saying that the two main countries which accept literary emigrants by numbers remain the U.S. and Canada. These countries should really be grateful to the Communist regimes for having sent them such talent.

It is interesting that you mention that, because I was just putting together a speech that I am supposed to deliver in Edmonton to a Czech society of arts and sciences, and I am comparing three literatures, the Czech, the American and the Canadian one. One of the things that I am mentioning in it is what has happened in Czechoslovakia during the past forty years, that there really hasn't been anybody of literary note, or intellectual note in the position of presidency over there. As a matter of fact, if they have one thing in common—the presidents they have had in Czechoslovakia—is that they are half-literates and unable to express themselves. They use this Marxist jargon and people roll their eyes and say, 'What the hell are they saying? What the hell do they mean?' And because there is nothing coming from the top which would indicate talent and great expressive ideas, it challenges the people to come up from the bottom. There is an awful lot of particularly (intelligent) people who are not in the government, the dissidents, and I think it strengthens them, because whatever the present guy over there, is singularly dumb. He is really just an *apparatchik* par excellence. He is, I think, an inspiration to the great dissident movement because I think anybody can be better.

If you look at your work, how much is purely, or partly ethnic background, and how much is Canadian?

I think it is a good idea to distinguish between background with specific locations as opposed to influence. I think the influence by where I have been, and where I have lived, goes all the way even into this nonfiction that I just produced, which is *Golden Revolution*. So far as fiction is concerned, there is no doubt that the first book, *Whatever Happened to Wenceslas?* started off in Europe and ends up on skid road in Vancouver, and in between we go through New York and a Southern University and pretty much followed places where I have been and where I have lived.

The next one, *Rosenkavalier*, is already half and half. Half of it takes place in Canada, in Vancouver specifically, and the other fifty percent in Czechoslovakia, and there is a much clearer comparison between the two and also the way it is put together. There is this moving back and forth. It is not that the first part of the book was in Europe and then the next one in North America.

The next one was a thriller, straight commercial stuff, and I had great fun writing it. *The Lister Legacy* is a story, to give you a background of it, of a Canadian naval commander who was dropped behind the enemy lines and falls in love with a beautiful Czech actress in World War II. Every chapter ends with sort of a cliff-hanger type of thing.

I was using background. For example the village where the big anti-Nazi action takes place was the same village where we used to spend all our summers in Czechoslovakia, so that one really stands apart a little bit.

Then comes the most serious thing that I have done so far. The book called *The Statement*, a political novel on an island in the Pacific called New Salisbury, which was mythical, but at moments looked an awful lot like New Zealand where I had spent some time researching the situation before I got down to writing it. Again, the whole plot takes place on this mythical island, and yet there was a great European influence in it. One of the main characters has European roots and arrives from Europe on this island, and there is a constant European influence there.

When it comes to the last one, which is nonfiction, it is fairly anecdotal and the anecdotes quite often come from my European background. You know there is a sort of a comparison that is thrown in here and there. I feel that it would be unnatural if I started acting, as you say, changing the name and becoming John Draybak instead of Jan Drabek and so started denying it consciously. I sort of let things go, and if I am writing about a particular subject, I say O.K., what do I have on that subject in the old brain and, like a computer, it starts spewing out ideas. Some of them have been there for fifty years. So, naturally, they have a European quality to them.

You are a member of The Writer's Union of Canada. Recently there was some correspondence in our Writers' Confidential— it has become some sort of movement that only a 'person of colour' could write about other 'persons of colour' and henceforth, we cannot write about Canadians because we only live here, we don't have the background. I read some thrillers by Canadian and American authors, set in Germany, specifically during the Second World War, and in one of them I find that just about everything he writes about is wrong. Background, names, everything. I get so irate that I can't finish them because not only have they not done their research, they don't have the background. What is your feeling about this?

There are some who do have it and who know where to go and get it, and there are others who stubbornly just wade in and decide that 'Because I am the great writer, people will accept what I say and I won't have to do research.' I know that in stamp collecting, and I am not a stamp collector, but one of the things that is great about the Protectorate of Bohemian Moravia is the so-called closed stamp collection. It has a beginning and it has an end, and it will never have any more stamps that will be added to it because it will, I hope, never exist again.

So, there you have a situation which would be rather difficult to penetrate unless you had actually lived there or unless you are writing a book about something else and you need a chapter that takes place during the time of Bohemian Moravia, you should take the trouble of going to speak to somebody and saying this is what I plan to do, and what should I be looking out for? Then when you write it, chances are that you should also have that chapter gone over by somebody who is familiar with Bohemian Moravia.

So far as writing about Canada is concerned, that is a much wider—what is Canada? I could not write about a Newfoundland fisherman. On the other hand, I could write about the mainstream Canadian because I have been living with one for twenty-five years, and she is a fourth-generation Canadian, I think, Canadian and Scottish-Irish, just strictly English speaking and sort of Anglo-Saxon oriented society. So I feel that I would be quite capable of writing about a native-born Canadian who has lived a life quite different from mine, and I also feel—and this is horror of horrors to some of those feminists who write in the Writers' Union Confidential pages—I could also write about a Canadian female. I would feel that I have been close enough to one to be able to write about that particular female. Now, I may not be able to write about the ones that have been writing these very radical feminist tracts in those pages, but maybe they are not as predominant as they think they are.

To what degree have the immigrant writers influenced or contributed to the state of excellence of Canadian writing?

Well, if you are talking about CanLit, I should say this very quietly, I have great reservations whether anything like CanLit actually exists. There are some competent writers. I don't think greatness has made a big appearance yet in Canadian writing. There are some competent writers and there are some very interesting writers.

I still have far to go to get into greatness. I think I am competent, yes. I don't think CanLit can be viewed as a literature with its own mythology. In the other two literatures, the one I studied in the States and the one into which I was born, in Czechoslovakia, they have certain qualities including time to sort of ripen, and in the case of the U. S. two hundred years, and in the case of Czechoslovakia something like six hundred. So, this is missing in Canadian literature, and I think there is—a little bit, not a little bit, a hell of a lot, and quite often you will hear it—an attempt to provide an instant type of literature. You know, pour a spoonful of this in hot water and you've got a literature.

So I, for example, do not see in Canada an involvement, a sort of intermingling of society and literature as such. They seem to exist on separate sides of the existence, and this is what disturbs me about it. I see the mythology is missing. There are no Siegfrieds in here. The closest thing to it is Louis Riel and (Dr. Norman) Bethune. The first one is really a simple act of divisiveness in Canada between the

French and English society, so we have trouble using him. The other one is greatly revered by the Chinese, but there are an awful lot of Canadians, despite the great things that he has done for medicine, (who dislike the fact) that he was an ardent Stalinist, Bethune. So, as a hero we are having problems there again.

Having been brought up in a situation where you have George Washingtons and Abraham Lincolns, being born into a culture where you have Wenceslas and Tomas Masaryk—all these people who just seem to have figured in the literature of the country—I am having trouble finding that kind of central point in Canadian literature, and so this is my problem so far as CanLit is concerned. I have sort of stayed away from discussions of it because I don't want to destroy the great enthusiasm that exists over here, but give me another twenty or thirty years and I will tell you whether CanLit is going great guns or not.

So, yes, there have been competent writers. I have again trouble in seeing Vizinczey and Skvorecky and (George) Faludy, for example, as contributors to a whole identifiable shape of Canadian literature. I see them as people who are writing in Canada, who are writing quite capably, who are writing from a different viewpoint, but as to whether they actually give shape to CanLit as such, I don't know. I am having trouble with that one. I am having trouble with CanLit between French and English speaking literature. I am having trouble even with West and East literary styles.

So, not knowing what CanLit really is, I am having trouble answering your question which goes, "What have these people contributed to it?"

Ajmer
Rodé

Surjeet
Kalsey

Surjeet Kalsey came to Canada from India in 1974, and has a master's degree in English and Punjabi literature from the Punjabi University in Chandigarh. She worked as a news broadcaster on All-India Radio for five years. At the University of British Columbia she got her master's degree in creative writing in 1978. She has published poems in a number of literary magazines in India and Canada, and has published one book of poetry in Punjabi as well as two in English. At present she is working as a full-time counsellor in a Transition House for battered women and children. Her literary works-in-progress are a collection of contemporary Canadian-Punjabi poetry and a collection of contemporary Canadian short fiction. Ms Kalsey is also a well known translator with many titles to her credit. She lives in Richmond, B.C.

Ajmer Rodé was born in a rustic Punjabi village in India on New Year's morning, 1940. He received his BA (Sc) from the Punjabi University and his MA (Sc) from the University of Waterloo after he immigrated in 1966. He has been living, since then, on the West Coast working mostly as an engineer. He started writing Punjabi poetry in his teens, greatly influenced by his older brother, Navtej, himself a poet. In his twenties his creative urges somewhat changed their form of expression, and science became his first love—he wrote his first book, in Punjabi, on the relativity theory—but in his thirties he returned to literature. Now he finds it hard to imagine life without writing. He writes both in Punjabi and English. Two books of poetry and two of plays have been published; two more books of poetry are ready for publication, and four manuscripts are in progress. He has been involved in literary and cultural activities since moving to Vancouver in the early seventies. In 1987 he was co-ordinator of the first Canadian-Punjabi literary conference held in Vancouver. He has been deeply involved in Punjabi theatre in B.C., having written, directed and acted in more than ten plays. He lives in Richmond, B.C.

JURGEN HESSE: Would you like to tell me something of your background?

SK: I came from Punjab fifteen years ago, and I got my education in Punjabi, and English too, before I came here.

AR: I was born in Punjab. *Punj* means five, and *ab* means waters. A very beautiful name. Five Waters. Land of Five Waters. I was born there in a village called Rodé. That is where I got my last name. I don't want to completely cut off myself from my background, so I assumed the name Rodé after coming here to Canada. I was Ajmer Singh before.

I was born into a real rural, rugged part of Punjab. Rodé is a village where—incidentally, the leader of Khalistan who initiated the whole thing—also comes from the same village. So that will give you some idea of where I come from. My father and grandfather, in fact I guess up to ten generations, lived there. And our generation— our means my brothers, my sister and myself—we were the first ones to go to school.

In the village?

AR: No, in the family. I was the first one to become an engineer from my village. I have some kind of first anyway. My essential bringing up was in the village of a rural area. Then, for secondary education I went to the city where I got my grades eleven and twelve, then to engineering (school) in the same city, one of our bigger cities in Punjab.

But I would like to mention something interesting, and that is the transition from the village to the city was at least as big or traumatic as coming from India to Canada for me. A real rural Punjab is quite different from the very urbanized Punjab.

Your working language was Punjabi . . . when did the English come?

AR: Oh, we started with English in fact in grade six, but it was one subject among many. However, it was the most important. We had to pass it to pass a grade. If you failed in English, you failed in everything and would have to repeat the grade. So it was tragic for many students who weren't good in languages. Some schools failed students three times, four times, just to do good English. I think it was the most dreaded language, but at the same time the most prestigious. I wasn't too bad. I was good in studies in general, and so I just didn't have that much problem.

But to me, that fact amounted to a criminal act. I get upset about it still, because some of my real good friends feared they would never pass beyond grade ten just due to this English. And they would never have used it. But it was almost criminal for the university, the government of the people who started this system. This would be in 1958.

You are saying then that a lot of your friends had their lives changed drastically because they couldn't pass the one subject?

AR: English. Well, math was also important, but it was mostly English. And the teaching of English was awful. The method, I think, was directly imported from England at that time. They would start teaching grammar in grade six. And that is what most students just could not do. So I have this love and hate.

The study of English was a very prominent aspect of our studies, and at the same time it was a window to the great literature. In grade eleven I read *War and Peace* in English, so it was only due to English that I could have access to these classics. And then we came to the city, to a very raw type of student and a very prestigious college, one of the top-most colleges in Punjab. A government college where only élite people would go. So I got admission due to my good marks. I was one of the better students.

At what age did you come here?

AR: I was twenty-six.

Did you and Surjeet know each other then?

AR: No. I went back. Well, most people go back for marriage, I went for something else. I stayed there for more than a year, and so we met and got married. A bit different from the arranged marriages.

Yes. Well, I am not after a romantic story here (Rodé laughs). When was your first exposure to writing? What made you write, and when?

AR: I think that the creative aspect has been always with me. I think from early childhood. My brother, he is two years older, he had exposure to the literary and arts world. He wrote poems when he was in grade seven, I guess even before that. So I guess that could be one reason why I picked up that, and he really influenced me heavily. He is a very talented and brilliant man. He is in London these days. But that could be just one of the factors. But somehow this creative aspect was always with me, even in grades six and seven. I took part in plays in the school, I read poems. All of it in Punjabi.

So English is truly your second language.

AR: Oh yes. Very much. Now I consider these two languages mine, but Punjabi is the one which is in my bones, not only the blood. Then I think I wrote a poem in grade nine, then in grade eleven and twelve, I also wrote a poem or two and a short story and got it published under somebody else's name. So it was with me, but what happened, I somehow got interested in the sciences, fundamental sciences.

Is writing a secondary occupation for you, or is it as valuable as your professional occupation?

AR: Now my love is writing. Of course most impotant is engineering because it feeds the family and myself. If I had a choice to leave my profession, I would leave it today, and I would phone tomorrow morning that I am not going to come in to work and that I am going to write twenty-four hours. Well, I probably would like to do that, but people who come from outside just cannot afford that luxury. Well, you have also come from outside, I know. But, people like us, we just cannot afford it. Maybe in India we could have done that, but here . . . . It would be very hard for us. I was in Victoria ten, twelve years ago, and I had friends before my marriage. I lived here for two or three years, and there, incidentally, the people I moved with were all from here. English-speaking writers, mostly writers and singers, the folk singer Valdy. They said they wished that I would leave (my work). Once I told them I was going to leave the university. I was working in the computer department there. And they were all glad. "Just leave that kind of trash," they said, "and do something creative." But we just can't afford it.

That is where I think already a hidden kind of racism comes. I don't think people would tolerate people coming from outside, like us, and depending on grants.

There would be a resentment?

AR: Resentment.

SK: You can't get a grant as a Punjabi writer. You can get it for English only, or translation, maybe.

AR: So while we would love to do full-time writing, we just can't do it.

In what language do you write now? When did you make the switch, or are you still writing in Punjabi?

AR: Both in Punjabi and English.

With which do you feel more comfortable?

AR: Punjabi. Well, of course there is not that much difference but still, it is Punjabi. There is a very subtle difference. Even though we have quite a bit of English and are quite comfortable with it now, when I use a word or an image in Punjabi, I can almost sense, gauge, an entire Punjabi-speaking audience of writers or non-writers. I know whether this image is new, or how it is going to be received. In English, I still can't see that fine impact of an image. Unless you are writing full-time or are totally immersed in writing in English . . . you have to have been here from your childhood on, I guess. But in spite of that, I think we can still make a valuable contribution.

Tell me a bit about that, what did you call it, invisible racism?

AR: Hidden racism, or whatever. I think there's a perception that people who come from outside, especially from Asian origin, are expected to work, I mean physical work . . .

Yeah, that's what I was told when I came here in 1958 . . .

AR: And you can see that people who come from the outside slip to the very bottom (of the social scale). People coming from outside here, if they say, "I am not going to work here, I am just going to live on grants and write, and do some artistic adventures," I don't feel secure that way. Although I have all the rights, they are not going to be tolerated, especially when you first come. Now it's different, I feel much more confident. It takes a while to realize that you also pay taxes and have all the rights. A few years.

Do you have a bone to pick with some Canadians about being condescending or patronizing to you?

AR: Sometimes you feel that, but not very much. Sometimes people are not even aware (of it). That's what I mean with hidden racism. They claim to be from a progressive political party, writers, and this literature, this so-called ethnic literature, the very fact there is a concept of mainstream literature and ethnic literature . . .

I am very deliberately not talking about ethnic writers but of immigrant writers, which is a totally different thing. What have you published in English here?

AR: One book of poetry, and there is another one ready. I have written many poems in English.

Has prose ever been of interest to you?

AR: A few essays, critical essays, but nothing of substance. Then there are some translations in Punjabi. I have published in India, a book of poetry in Punjabi and two books of plays, and I have at least as much unpublished material. Four plays, and two books in Punjabi.

If we look at CanLit, thirty years ago it wasn't going far. Since then, much has happened in Canadian literature. How do you see the contribution of immigrant writers to CanLit?

AR: I still don't see that it has impacted very much. It's still the

so-called mainstream literature when we talk of Canadian literature
. . . Margaret Atwood, Pierre Berton, Earle Birney, and Al Purdy. I
don't know, there was one woman writer, she migrated to the
United States, her name is Mukherjee. You can call her a very
successful writer.

*I feel that immigrant writers have made a contribution here, although they
may have been seen as immigrant writers. Is that role going to expand?*

AR: Yes. It will. As time passes, a lot of people are more confident,
they can see their contributions as valuable. If we go out to a
reading, now I can see the audience responding. Not somebody
coming to tell you that it was nice, and it was good. It has been very
difficult for me to find out where my writing stands. It was very hard.
I had good friends, writers, but still I would be kind of suspicious of
their opinions if they would say, "It's very good."

Are people too polite?

AR: Probably. Andy Schroeder has been a good friend. He's the first
one when he read some of my poems, and of one of the poems he
said, "I didn't expect such trash from you." I think that was great.

Was he justified?

AR: Yeah. He argued that it was trash. I liked that. That was the first,
then about the other he said, "Those are nice images." But then I
had other friends who would say, "This is nice," and this and that,
and sometimes they were honest and sincere, but I always felt in the
dark. Where does my writing stand?

But I also have a friend, Michael Bullock, and when I showed
him a manuscript, a children's poem, he said, "Well, they won't
accept that in English." Now we have friends who can say what they
feel. However, now I learned that one of the publishers from
England is very interested in that (laughs).

*You have to ask at least three people for their opinion. A negative opinion can
be very crushing.*

AR: Oh, yes, I almost threw it away. And now, a Punjabi writer friend
of mine took it to England, and he passed it on to a publisher who
was delighted and passed it on to Oxford University. I don't think

they will publish it, but the very fact that they took time to look at it is very interesting.

This is something we want (honest criticism), then we will be able to judge where our writing stands. This has started to come now.

In what way has your writing been influenced by the Canadian experience?

AR: Quite a bit. Now, when I write in English, I just think of the Canadian environment. I have been here twenty-two years. I *feel* for the people here, I *feel* for the environment being damaged.

You're acquiring Canadian concerns.

AR: Yeah, I have. These problems bother me.

Anglo-Saxon writers appear to bury their passion behind a stony façade; they keep their emotion well in check. And yet, when the best of them write about emotions, it clashes like thunder. It's all there. Where does it come from? Where are your passions? Are they visible?

AR: Quite visible. Punjabis, especially, are very open to express their emotions. They won't be much different from Italians or Germans or French. I stayed with Germans when I came to Canada. Without really pretending anything, including India, she was my best landlady. Her kids used to stick around me. I wore a beard and a turban. Punjabis are very open in their expression of passion.

It's very striking for people who come from the Punjab or from India. It's very hard to find the essence of something. If you are going for a job interview, for instance, it's impossible for us to know whether the compliments paid to you mean something or whether it's a façade. It's very unsettling.

SK: You never find out what's going on in a person's mind.

Why is it that this was British Canada—this Anglo-Saxon surface layer is still very much in place? I wonder whether your children, for instance, will have the same kind of outwardly bland behavior . . .

AR: I think that is changing, Jurgen, that kind of Anglo-Saxon . . . dominance layer is probably being punctured quite fast as I see it. There are so many immigrants from different parts.

Are you going to write about this?

AR: Maybe. For our children to be raised in this culture, it's not their choice, so, they are forced to live here. If they're going to suffer, they're going to suffer not due to their own choice. And that disturbs me quite a bit.

You said the environmental concerns are becoming yours too. Do you feel you might become a cultural nationalist as so many of my writing colleagues are?

AR: In fact, I am to some extent, from the Canadian point of view. I am very much against Free Trade. Any American or multinational influence I reject. I don't like it.

Now I would like to switch to you, Surjeet. Do you have some observations?

SK: I have experienced that people do ask us the question, "Why do you write in English?" And that question sometimes is the same question as . . . perhaps we should be writing only in Punjabi about your culture. It annoys me, if a writer feels comfortable writing in English. And the next question is usually, "Who do you think your audience is?" The same question in a different way.

I am interested in motivations and limitations and skeletons in the closet— real or imagined. What do you write?

SK: I write poetry and short stories and I do translations. I have published three books, two in English and one in Punjabi. Ajmer writes plays, and then we perform them together. One play we wrote together. He directed, and I helped. As far as poetry goes, it's very private. Short stories, yes, we share them in *Canadian Fiction Magazine.*

We keep hearing that poetry is not being read, that the only market for it is either your own cultural group or special interest groups, or university students. Is that true?

SK: As far as our own community goes, it's not true. People do enjoy poetry. In India there is a (poetry-reading) tradition, with huge audiences. I visited India last December, and I got the audience there. Here too. When I started translating before going into English, that was when I joined Creative Writing (at UBC) in 1974, at that time Ajmer and I said that we would try to put together poetry readings in both languages. Most of the audience were students and writers. It continued for four to five years.

It's not surprising that here (in Canada) is such a small audience for serious fiction. In your country (India) and mine (Germany) the tradition of fiction and poetry goes back hundreds and hundreds of years.

SK: Fifteen years ago I found that people were not familiar with Punjabi literature here, that professors and students at university didn't even know that it existed. Those were the years when I was a student at UBC.

My anthology was ready in 1978, and then I started sending it to the publishers. One of them, Intermedia Press (in Vancouver), really liked it and wanted to publish it. They accepted it in 1978, and we signed a contract. I was so excited and Ajmer was, too. It was a huge anthology of Punjabi poetry, first time to be published in Canada. And it was side-by-side bilingual. They applied for a grant, got it from the Secretary of State, then we went over the proofs, got the Punjabi typesetting from India, we laid out everything, the blueprints were ready, and then, after that, they said, "We don't want to publish it."

What happened with the book?

SK: I wrote that, since they were not going to publish it, I would take my manuscript back. One day, a Special Delivery came to my house, a big package, and I knew those were the blueprints. I didn't accept them. The publisher phoned me and said he wrote to the Secretary of State department that he was selling me the manuscript for three thousand dollars or something, settling the grant from the Secretary of State through me. So I didn't take the blueprints but took my manuscript. Now the reputed Literary Academy of Punjab is willing to publish it.

Almost every writer has a similar story to tell. Make an educated guess why you think they didn't go with it.

SK: One thing was, they thought they weren't going to get any readers. That they could not sell it. Purely economic, though we assured them that five hundred copies would be sold, at a minimum. The poetry was so different, so nice.

AR: If the writer had been born here, she would have found another way. That's one of the immigrant's problems. So much work was done.

SK: These were well-established Punjabi writers. And Punjabi is a beautiful language, very simple, very soft.

AR: The thirteenth-largest language (in the world).

I was asking you about skeletons in your closet. What are the things that really irritate you here as a writer?

SK: We are getting readings from different organizations. Last year we have done a lot of them. Organizations are getting grants for them. Last time I felt that these people are using us to get their grants. Using us, the immigrants, the native Indians, and the disabled. Put everything together, and they get the grant. What we experienced was that they give one hundred fifty dollars to one writer, one hundred to another, fifty to another. They knew that they weren't going to be cross-checked. The same writers are reading together time and time again, and one time it all got out into the open.

Do you have any opinion of the Secretary of State's Multiculturalism Branch?

SK: We don't know about them, because they are in Ottawa. They are funding who can write a wonderful grant application, and who can justify that application. And who can write that? The people with an English background, the people who know everything—

No, no, not just people who write English well. I know how it's done.

*   Can you take a look at Canadian Literature, and tell me how well it is placed in relation to world literature? Are we Canadian writers world class?*

SK: A little bit, not much. Al Purdy and Earle Birney were known (to us) as American writers. Canadian Literature does not have its own identity, yet. Now it's more influenced by the Americans. It might come, but it might not. They get more easily published in America than in Canada now, these days. At the last (Canadian writers') conference I attended there were agents from American publishers who were telling writers how to get published easily and fast in America.

AR: I don't think Canadians have produced a classic of their time, like French and Russian fiction, even from Indian and Bengali writers.

I wonder if it's the (right) time for writing milestones of literature. Many talents are wandering off to the flesh pots, going to Hollywood, writing screen drama, becoming, if you'll pardon the expression, hacks.

AR: That has something to do with the general environment. These are a different kind of setting. Everybody is sitting around, getting published, discussing movie rights. In that kind of environment it's hard that something like *Crime and Punishment* would be written.

SK: I meet writers at these readings, and I think we are not in the stream. Immigrant writers, I mean. That would be just a judgment when I say that I cannot find anything which strikes me, so far, in the mainstream. I think our literature still stands out as immigrants' literature. It is not the same as English literature.

Is it because of the subjects or because of what you are?

SK: I think partially because of what we are, and sometimes because of the subjects. They find they like it, or they found it different, so that is why they like it. I think I am just mentioning Indo-Canadian writers. We as Punjabi writers, not just as all immigrants. Can you ask any easy questions?

I cannot transport myself into your skin. I would like to know what it is like to be discriminated against, or seen in a different light.

SK: I think we still have something to hold onto, because I still like writing in Punjabi. Which is our own language, right? There is nothing to lose. So if we are writing in English it is just a pleasure to write in English. We are not struggling to write in English. Especially I am not. Because if it is coming in English, that is fine, and if people like it that is fine. If they don't, we still have something to hold onto.

(to AR) You were disagreeing I think, with your wife, or did I misread you there?

AR: No, I don't think so. We were talking about Canadian literature in perspective.

SK: No he was saying the same thing. That Canadian (literature) is seen as American literature in the outside world.

AR: We are not as knowledgeable as we should be to make that statement.

In Germany and in Italy, the countries that I know quite well, they have uncles in America even if they are from Canada. It is America. The whole thing here is America. I suppose it's more of a geographical term including all of North America.

AR: Well, when I was going to come for the first time to Canada, I went to the library just to look for books of Canadian literature so that I would be familiar with the Canadian literacy. All I found was one book that was written by—what is Trudeau's comrade, the guy who wrote the book . . . . There is a French writer. Trudeau and he co-authored a book, *Two Innocents In Red China.* Anyway, there was only one book, and it was commissioned by Trudeau and that French writer, and that was all. It was a pretty dead library.

Twenty-two years ago?

AR: Yes. So, I could read a lot about geography, but there was nothing on literature.

Now of course there is very much, the libraries have identified all the books that are Canadian with flags on them.

AR: In India I'm not sure if it has gone that far or not.

SK: No I think they are teaching American literature in the English department. I took an American literature course.

AR: Yes I know, but that was a while ago.

SK: Even now. Because they might have included some writers from Canadian literature, but Canadian literature I don't see.

AR: It doesn't stand as a big literature. But I got a letter from a friend who had done a play by a Canadian writer and dramatist. He is a very famous one, the one who wrote *The Ecstasy of Rita Joe.*

George Ryga. He died last year.

AR: Yes he died. And they just wrote me to pass on to him that he has been done in Punjabi. I could not reach him. I just phoned Avon Books, and I don't know if they gave him the message or not.

So, they are being recognized now, the Canadian writers.

SK: Presently I am doing two projects with the Secretary of State (Department). One is *Contemporary Canadian-Punjabi* short stories and the *Canadian Contemporary Punjabi Poetry.*

Is this something that is going to be published for certain?

SK: Yes. Well, I got the grant on these two. I have been working on this.

English-Canadian writers who never had to struggle with a second language have the same problem as everyone else, and that is to get publishers to listen. This is a world-wide problem, especially in view of the mergers and the horrible spectre of takeovers. A gasoline company is buying a publishing house! A clothes merchant buys the largest Canadian publisher! And nobody really talks about it, 'How the hell did you get in here? What makes you a literary expert?' The outsiders are coming in and treating us as if we were a piece of chewing gum.

AR: I don't think we disagree on that. It is terrible. It is really terrible. In fact I made a statement that I am a nationalist. Well, I think nationalism is abused, and I am not a nationalist from that point of view, but if a country is being victimized then I have every right to be a nationalist. In the same way, if an ethnic minority is victimized, then I will stand forward and identify myself as a Sikh, as an Indian, or whatever. But if it is not, then I have no reason to champion a separate cause. The same with nationalism.

But at the moment I think I don't hide myself, calling myself a nationalist. As you say with these takeovers and the American influence, we (really) have no right to say that they are bad.

SK: Oh, they are not. They are successful.

AR: No, but the culture, the values of extreme materialism and the influence of capitalism—let me go that far—is horrendous, and we don't want any part of it coming here. There are the good points and bad points, but, if we look at the present American society, the end product of capitalism and democracy, I am not for that. So we don't want that part spilling over to Canada.

We write for our own pleasure, but we also feel that what we have written should really be published if we think it is good, because we would like other people to share in the product of our mind. How do we know? Or don't we write for readers?

SK: Again, it depends on what kind of readers. So, it depends on what kind of pains you have, or I have, or someone else has.

Pains?

SK: Pains, I am talking about pains. It is hard to say who are the readers.

So we are working in a vacuum.

AR: Especially immigrant writers. It is a very very important question we are talking about. It is a universal question, suggestive of all literature types.

SK: Yes, if you look at the pains of these writers . . . I don't know if you are introducing the pains or not in your book, from the literature. From actual original versions.

Samples of immigrant writings? No.

SK: No, you are not?

No, this is purely anecdotes and opinions. I want the writers to speak.

SK: For example, I have written about farm-worker women. How they come here and how they have to go straight to the farms to work. To the Richmond, Abbotsford, Langley, Surrey, Delta areas. And that is the easiest way to find the job or work when they come from India or from the Punjab because they don't speak any English, and they don't need any English on the farms. But it is hard work, and they have never done this work before, most of them. They accept this work just because of lack of English.

I would bet that most Canadians think these farm-working women do the same kind of work in the Punjab.

SK: No, they don't. Actually, most of them have never worked in the fields before.

AR: About ninety-five per cent have not.

SK: Yes. Some of them are very young girls, or young women. Maybe newly, or only married for a few years, and they have a good education but they cannot function here. They are new. They have no Canadian experience. They have no English, and right away when they come to Canada that is the easiest way to find work. So these kinds of pains are in my poetry and in my short stories. It is kind of making a part of the history of the immigrant literature.

You would have a bigger impact if you wrote for newspapers or magazines, like MacLean's, Saturday Night, The Globe and Mail, *and the weekend papers. You know that of course.*

SK: Yes. I do write articles in Punjabi for our own community, but I think that is not my writing.

I find this very important, that these women are well educated and working at manual labor in the fields, under the hot sun, and probably underpaid.

SK: And long hours. Like ten or eleven hours a day.

I didn't know, and now I can no longer be ignorant about this. How can a reporter, fresh out of journalism school, who hears about trouble in the strawberry fields here with the farm workers—how can he report accurately about what is going on, without speaking Punjabi? In the first place, he doesn't have a clue who these people are who work in the fields. How can we expect him to give an accurate reading of what is happening if he doesn't know the cultural background?

SK: Interesting. Now I will tell you, I agree with this. The Farm Workers Union, last year they decided to make a video on pesticide. Again this was the problem if they hired a professional video maker, Canadian, white, then they don't know the language. They don't know the culture. So they need someone who can work with them. Someone who knows the language, knows the culture. Then, as they did last year, they hired me as a writer. I worked with the video makers, two women. One was the photographer, and the other was the director. I went into the fields, I worked with her, I wrote the script, everything. Everything was ready, and then I got sick last year, and I could not go on. So what happened? She wrote everything out of that. Made the film. And it was presented as *her* video.

And she is Anglo-Saxon?

SK: Right. They didn't even mention that I worked with them for four months, in the fields, interviewing people, and gave all the cultural backgrounds, everything.

Was the video accurate?

SK: Well, yes. Because in most of the scenes I was there. I actually directed scenes, and I talked to the farm workers in Punjabi, gave them directions on how to do this and that, and the scenes are accurate because I was there on the spot and was half directing, co-directing in Punjabi.

How do you see this?

SK: I see this as something that happened which is unfair. But I accept it myself because I fell sick at that time.

But even so, a credit had to be given, really. That is probably not too unusual.

SK: And they agreed to pay me something. They did not pay me. So everything was gone. I found out that they were struggling to put their names as directors, writers, and that kind of thing—competitiveness. They could not have done this video if one of us had not helped.

But the thing is, again, I want to make this point here that if we are writing in our own language, Punjabi, we are adding something to our own literature, to Punjabi literature, which I think is nowadays beginning to be introduced into the university—Canadian-Punjabi literature—in the Punjab. So they are recognizing (our writing) as part of the Punjabi literature, as a separate stream, but part of Punjabi literature. But what we are writing in English, well, that might be working in a vacuum, maybe. But then, again, it might be that after twenty, thirty or fifty years, it could be added to the history of Canadian-Punjabi literature. It might be seen as immigrant literature, as you emphasize, and it might be written by immigrants, but still it will show up the history.

Yes, of course, it is going to be a part of Canada, Canadian history.

Henry Kreisel

Henry Kreisel was born in Vienna, Austria in 1922, and came to Canada in 1940. He studied English literature at the University of Toronto (BA, MA), and later at the University of London (PhD). Since 1947 he has been on the staff of the University of Alberta where he became head of the department of English in 1961 and later served as senior associate dean of graduate studies from 1967 to 1970 and as vice-president (academic) from 1970 to 1975. In 1975 he was given the rank of university professor. That year he was invited to be a Visiting Fellow of Wolfson College at the University of Cambridge. Dr. Kreisel has held a number of major offices in provincial and national organizations, among them president of the Association of Canadian University Teachers of English, and chairman of the Canada Council Postgraduate Committee for English literature. He has also served on the Governor-General's Award Jury for literature and was a member of the board of governors of the University of Alberta.

Henry Kreisel is the author of two novels, *The Rich Man* (McClelland and Stewart, Toronto, 1948) and *The Betrayal* (McClelland and Stewart, 1964); a collection of short stories, *The Almost Meeting* (NeWest Press, Edmonton, 1981); and *Another Country: Writings by and about Henry Kreisel* (NeWest Press, 1985), edited by Professor Shirley Neuman. His major contribution to Canadian literature has been to bridge two worlds—the European and the Canadian. The poet Miriam Waddington has commented on "the ease with which he moves between Canadian and European landscapes." His work has been recognized by major awards, notably the President's Medal of the University of Western Ontario, the J.L. Segal Foundation Award for literature, and the Sir Frederick Haultain Prize, awarded to him by the government of Alberta for significant contributions to the fine arts. In 1987 he was made an Officer of the Order of Canada. He lives in Edmonton, Alberta.

JURGEN HESSE: I presume you're an older-generation writer?

HENRY KREISEL: I'm sixty-seven now. I came here in 1940. I left Austria, went to England, was interned and sent to Canada with a group of people, many of whom you may have heard of. My book reprints a diary that I kept of my internment. There's a group of six, seven hundred who came over. Many of us were then released here in Canada, went to school, or did other things. I studied English at the university. My book describes how I became a writer, my attitude to language, the change of language and what this meant, which is in an essay that has been reprinted many times.

When did you discover writing?

In Austria, in school. I wrote in German then. I made the decision here in the internment camp that I would become an English writer. I had some idea about what this meant, and the difficulties. I talk about this in an essay called, *Language and Identity.* I discuss the problem of changing languages in more than simply my own case but try to see it in the psychological context, particularly of (Joseph) Conrad.

The influence on me by A.M. Klein, the great Jewish poet, Montreal poet, was decisive. He showed me how one could use one's background and one's heritage in a way that would make it possible for one to be a complete writer. So you have to take on the kind of identity to make yourself over in the image of the people to whom you wanted to speak. These are the two great influences in my life. This is the major milestone in my life, perhaps the central event of my life, when I made the decision to become a writer in English. That led to certain steps that I took. I began to study English literature because I wanted to know the tradition, the background of the language, immerse myself in the language. It led then to my entering a program in English language and literature. I stuck to it and had, in fact, a very distinguished academic career in Toronto.

I was first in first class honors four years straight and then did a master's degree. Then I came to Alberta in 1947 as a junior lecturer, went off to London to do my PhD, and then came back again. I certainly didn't think of my academic career when I made the decision to write in English, but that's how it turned out. My writing and my academic career are thus very closely linked, and in fact my doctoral thesis in London was on exile and alienation. It was a thesis more than an academic exercise for me, an attempt to understand the forces in the modern world that led to exile, to alienation, which was not then a very popular word. It has since become an *in* word. When I did my thesis in fifty-two, it wasn't a word much used. I used it because I had an understanding of the processes of changing cultures, of changing environments, of changing languages. So I used my thesis to understand my own situation even though I was talking essentially about Conrad. Conrad was one of the major figures, and James Joyce, and Virginia Woolf, and D.H. Lawrence. These were the major figures I discussed in my thesis.

Both my Austrian, my Jewish, my Canadian experience could be welded together to form a whole.

I would like to compare your career with that of Peter Newman. Newman came from Czechoslovakia at the age of ten.

I know Peter. He came in a different way. As an immigrant.

As far as I know, Peter Newman has never really referred to the fact that he is an immigrant. He became a quintessentially English-Canadian writer, whereas you say that you have drawn very much on your past experiences. Would you hazard a guess as to why Peter Newman has chosen that route?

I really can't venture to speak for him. His writing is somewhat different. He does not write fiction. I think the psychological makeup is somewhat different. He saw himself, to begin with, as a reporter rather than a novelist. The use of material that one chooses is different, it comes from a different level of consciousness, of unconsciousness. The fact that he was only ten would make a difference. I was already, to some extent, formed. Not as much as, say, somebody like (Josef) Skvorecky, who was older. I was young enough, but at the same time old enough, to have been immersed in another tradition, the tradition of Austrian and German literature, and of Jewish literature which I knew quite well.

So I knew these influences, and to some extent the forms of my fiction derived from the tradition of the German novella, which is a form not much analyzed in English. In German it is a form that has been much studied as practised by Thomas Mann, and by (his brother) Heinrich Mann. I knew the English tradition as well.

My master's thesis is on American literature. I have never taught Canadian literature, but I have written on it. A number of traditions thus combined to form what I think has become my work. I had a real sense of standing between two worlds and looking back from Canada at Europe, and looking from Europe to Canada. I was quite conscious of that situation, of that way of looking.

Can you guess, or assess, whether the people who were born in Canada— the readers of books who have no direct, first-hand knowledge of life in Europe or elsewhere—are interested in literature such as you have written?

Some are, obviously. I have a small but steady readership. All my work is still in print. My first novel was published in 1948. I think it still sells something like ten thousand copies a year. It's on curricula in schools.

You said you studied Canadian literature. It was not so much on the map then, in the forties and fifties.

That's right, absolutely. My essay goes into that—*Has Anyone Here Heard Of Marjory Pickthall?* It's in that book, *Another Country*.

Are you excited about the new generation of immigrant writers such as Michael Ondaatje?

Yes, I am, and particularly about the new strain that is coming in. Ondaatje is sort of halfway house.

Rohinton Mistry . . .

Yes, and the Indian writers that have come in. And people of Japanese extraction—Joy Kogawa. I am very excited about that new stream that's feeding into the mainstream. That will enrich Canadian literature in a new way because, after all, Canadian literature, from the beginning, was like American literature, originally an offspring of European literature. The early writers were essentially European writers living in Canada, even though they may have been born here. The forms are all nineteenth-century romantic and post-romantic forms of poetry and of prose. These people have been a pervasive influence, and that still remains, even with writers from Asia. They bring a new kind of consciousness, a new kind of approach to fiction. Their consciousness has been formed in other than European countries. I think we will be seeing a new way of looking at things.

In general, of course, what's been happening in Canada since the sixties is quite amazing, the outburst of creativity that we're seeing, and no one could have foreseen that. It was often people, outsiders like myself, who saw the possibilities in Canadian literature, and were attracted to it. We were outsiders and were quite astonished to find how much interest there was.

Alberto Manguel

Alberto Manguel was born in Buenos Aires in 1948, and after years of travel he came to Canada in 1982, and became a Canadian citizen in 1988. He was educated at the Colegio de Buenos Aires, at the Universidad de Buenos Aires, Letras, and at London University. He is the author of numerous books, including *The Dictionary of Imaginary Places*, and has written some six plays. His work has also appeared in numerous periodicals and magazines in Canada, Britain, and the United States. He works as a fiction reviewer and editor in Toronto, has been a reader in Paris and London, was a reporter, foreign editor, and editor-in-chief of various newspapers, and even sold books in Argentina. He also translates mostly from Spanish and French into English, as well as works by Sylvia Plath into Spanish. He is fluent in English, Spanish, French, German, and Italian, and can read Swedish and Portuguese. He lives in Toronto.

JURGEN HESSE: Can you tell me something about your experiences before coming to Canada?

ALBERTO MANGUEL: I was born in Argentina but I moved immediately to Israel because my father was the Argentinian ambassador in Israel. I never learned Hebrew, but I had a Czech nanny who taught me German and English, so those were my first languages, really. I came back to Argentina at the age of seven and learned Spanish at that point and stayed in Argentina until I was eighteen, then moved around, travelled in Europe, lived in the South Pacific, and at the end of 1982 came to Canada.

When was the first impulse for you to write?

Very early, I suppose, as anyone who is interested in books at the age of seven or eight. I would already write stories and plays for public theatres, because I was brought up by this nanny who had curious ideas about education. She had the idea that you should know everything in life before the age of seven. So she taught me all sorts of bizarre things before then. By that time I already was writing. I can remember a play for the public theatre which had Christ and Moses discussing things. Then I wrote only sporadically.

At the age of eighteen, just before I left Argentina, I won a literary prize with a newspaper there. Immediately after that I decided I wouldn't write anymore. I have always been very interested in books, and I tried going to university and studied literature at Buenos Aires University, but I found that very boring. I started reading the things I wanted to read.

I felt I would never write as well as the people I really enjoyed. So I decided I wouldn't write anymore, and in fact didn't write until just before I came to Canada. This was at the end of 1982. Just before that, at the end of 1981, I had set up a small publishing company that didn't work and went bankrupt. This was in England. One of the projects I had which had come from a friend of mine was to compose *The Dictionary of Imaginary Places*. At first I thought this would (mean to) be working as an editor, a publisher, just helping my friend putting things together, but it turned out that in the end I did most of the writing because he wanted only to tackle the Italian part and the Russian literature. I tackled the others. We ended up with a book that is really enormous, the size of a phone book. That book worked out.

When did you start (writing) again, at what age?

Let me see, eighty-one, I was born in forty-eight, so that is at age thirty-three.

So you had a hiatus of about fifteen years. That is very unusual.

But I read a lot. My feeling has always been that you can tackle literature from either side, just be a reader, (which is) as important as being a good writer, training yourself to be a good reader.

From this comes the course that you are at present teaching here at Simon Fraser University in Vancouver.

I don't really know what the course is going to be until we finish it (laughs). Canada really offered me an opportunity I didn't think I would have. I worked in literary surroundings in Paris, in Italy, in England, mainly with publishing companies and meeting many writers. Sort of living in a literary milieu. I never felt my opinions as an outsider really counted much. To be a writer in Paris, an immigrant writer, you have to have cheek, and I don't. I didn't really try very hard, but in Canada it was very strange. I arrived at the end of eighty-two, in October, and by November I was reviewing for the *Globe and Mail.* This was simply through a series of phone calls, but it wasn't an isolated case. There seemed to be a generous spirit in the way things are done. I was surprised that they would let me try. I had no experience in writing. It's one of the few cases I know of where you are tried out. I started writing for American papers because I was writing for Canadian papers. The most absurd thing was when I got a phone call from the New York Times, asking me if I would review a book, and I said sure. But where did they get my name? "Oh well," they said, "we read reviews, and we read your reviews about books in Canada."

I am very grateful for people like yourself who have paved the way from the sixties onward. I arrived when everything was much easier and better said.

When you look at Canadian literature, do we have world-class writers?

I think we do. Now. Certain things are world-class, perhaps certain books by certain writers are world class. Margaret Atwood's *The Handmaid's Tale.* Findley's *The Wars,* and *Not Wanted On the Voyage,* especially. And Michael Ondaatje, most of his work. Robertson Davies. They are world class. But we are still a very shy literature. There is no publicity around Canadian literature. It's almost not necessary for a writer to make a name outside the country. When it happens, as in the case of Atwood, it's almost by chance because it's been picked up by a certain group.

In other cases, for instance French or Japanese literature, it's important for a writer to become known outside. It happens, then writers become important outside the country. For Canadian literature that hasn't happened. They have all been very badly published outside. That's part of the problem.

And yet we have courses in Canadian literature, for instance in Bologna . . .

Yes. I don't know that that does very much. I think it remains part of the academic world and doesn't go beyond.

When you say "shy literature," are you saying what many Canadians are saying, that we are almost afraid to show our mettle, to show that we are good and can compete?

Yes, I think so. In literature as well. It's difficult to make these suppositions because you have no facts to base them upon. But if an Italian had written *The Wars*, we would be hearing about *The Wars* in every country in the world. *The Wars* has been published in a number of languages, and there is nothing to push it.

Tell me about your own writing. Where is it going? Do you get anything out of Canada except that it is now your new home?

In my case, the relationship with Canada was important and exciting, because I was suddenly being faced with a curious audience, having taught the difference of coming into a class(room) where people look bored and look at the watch and want to leave, and others who have expectant faces and are really wanting to hear what you have to say. It's very flattering and makes you nervous, but at the same time it's exciting and makes you want to work. What happened here was that I suddenly felt there are people who listen to what I have to say. That made me think more carefully what I wanted to say. That let me have the sort of courage I need to launch into fiction. I am trying to write a novel, like everybody else.

I don't know whether that would happen somewhere else. That's the point. It has a lot to do with the interest and curiosity that provokes that kind of expectation. Part of it is invented, of course. You think that you have an interested, captive audience, and in fact it is somebody who is trying to look beyond (you) at the door to see what time it is. *(Laughs.)* I started working for the CBC, and I was very flattered because *Ideas* (a long-running series of one-hour radio documentaries) asked me to put together a program, and then I was on *Morningside* (another long-running magazine-format radio program with host Peter Gzowski) doing things. Then a producer on *Morningside* said, "The reason we really want you on *Morningside* is because of your accent."

(Laughs) Things have really changed at the CBC, I tell you . . .

Now if you have a British accent, it's no good. He was trying to be very nice, you see. Of course if I were saying exactly the same things but my accent were an Oxford accent, would I be allowed on the radio? The answer seems to be no. What I am saying doesn't seem to matter but for the tone, not even how I say it, but the tone.

I live in the East End of Vancouver where people tend to display bulging biceps with tattoos on their arms. This is the poor area. By and large, Danielle Steel and others, this kind of book seems to be their favourite. The poorer part of the population is vastly larger than the well-educated, especially the Toronto suburbanite. Is there not a danger that literature in Canada appeals only to the cognoscenti, the educated?

I suppose that is a danger which exists everywhere. I think it's even more dangerous to equate an interest in good literature—what I mean by that is challenging literature—with the upper classes. It lends the idea of the intellectual a social connotation as something superfluous or exploitative that it doesn't have. We hear too much now that things are too intellectual, too literary, too élitist, and the CBC reflects that. They tend to lower the level of everything and over-explain everything and make things far less interesting that way.

There is a danger of looking at literature on a social scale. Also it doesn't reflect the truth anyway, because occasionally I have done readings for groups and for certain clubs, and my experience is the people who don't have the means to buy hardcover books are nevertheless interested and want to be challenged. We have to talk here about the differences between the classes in Canada and of the differences in the classes anywhere else. What we mean by somebody poor, not affluent, in Canada, is probably a person who is well off in Uruguay.

We're still talking about people (here) who have a number of advantages. We know there is illiteracy—both absolute and functional—in Canada, we know there are homeless people in Canada, we know there are people for whom the priority is to eat rather than to read Shakespeare. But, nevertheless, we still live in Canada in a society where things are much, much, much better than in a number of other places. The means for those people to have access for a more challenging culture are there.

Joseph Conrad was one of the first writers I know about who wrote in an adopted language. The other was Rainer Maria Rilke. In those days it was seen to be almost an impossibility to write expressively at the same quality level. How is it in your case?

In my case it's different, it's not that I speak English and German—my first languages—very fluently. I'd say that I am not entirely fluent in any language. They have come to me in such peculiar ways. In order for a person to be entirely fluent in a language you have to live in that language and make mistakes. I don't. My mistakes in English come from not knowing how to pronounce words that I have read and haven't heard pronounced. I learned English from my Czech nanny, and I learned to put all my verbs at the end of the sentence.

One of the major mistakes I find I make is that I have a keener eye for grammar than the people who speak English (from birth), and therefore the mistake we make is that we don't make many mistakes. I still will not use 'was' in the conditional. I'm reluctant to drop prepositions. I will *write 'to' somebody*, not *write somebody*. There are things you have to unlearn, perhaps.

When you have to write the way people speak—that's the hardest thing to do. I admire a great many dialogue writers—not on television, though. Does your novel deal with your experiences here in Canada?

It touches upon Canada. The reason I'm writing it, and this maybe would explain my relationship with Canada, is that my intention was not to write a novel ("Now let's see what story I can tell . . ."), which is how a number of people do write novels. The way I came to this novel is different. I left Argentina before the seventies, so I didn't go through the terrible military dictatorship of the seventies, but a number of my friends were there and stayed. Some were killed, others managed to leave.

During my time in high school, we had the influence of one teacher in particular who was very important and who introduced literature to us in a way that he made (us) feel we could live with it. It was my main impulse to live with books. At the end of the seventies, I met one of my friends who had escaped to Brazil, and he told me that this teacher had been found guilty of collaborating with the military dictatorship. In fact, that he had a very strong hand in providing information that led to (the) torture of friends of ours, (people) who had been his students.

I found myself with a very painful question: The person who I had felt had such a great influence on my life was in fact a monster. I didn't know how to deal with this.

And the book title, is it going to be something like The Monster?

Yes, *The Monster.* That led to the novel. I thought that perhaps (a novel) can explore the sort of thing that nonfiction could not. I would have to get too many facts (otherwise).

The external life experiences of many immigrant writers have been, compared with many of Canadian-born writers, paradisiacal. Does it matter to the quality of literature how much suffering a writer has been through?

I suppose that a writer transforms any experience into writing, and that experience need not be suffering. It can be some kind of happiness as well. It seems that it is usually suffering, but that is the case of almost every human being. The writer is not very different in that case. If you are asking whether I think the Canadian writer, because fewer things happened to that writer, has got less to transform into literature, I think that yes in the sense that it must be more difficult for somebody to whom very little has happened outside his consciousness—I mean physical stuff . . .

I'm thinking of Robertson Davies, for example . . .

Yes, the curious thing is, if you look at plot, at stories in Canadian literature, he's one of the ones who's got most of them. So they do live somewhere. If literature can provide it, if literature feeds literature, you can be a great reader and that will provide material for you to write. What is perhaps still lacking is a confidence in looking beyond Canada.

If you take, for instance, a French writer, nobody has to tell a French writer that he had a tradition. That's what you're born with. It's taken for granted. Nobody instructs that writer to follow a tradition in any way. That writer can sit down and write about Greece and about Latin America, and write about the moon. It just becomes part of the French tradition. Nobody asks any questions.

The Canadian writer believes, and I think this is what we have been saying about changes, up to a certain point, that there is a kind of obligation to touch upon things Canadian, that it must somehow give importance to the surroundings. It's a kind of literary nepotism. You have to sort of give your nephew an important kind of position in the government. Well, you don't. The best kind of people can come from elsewhere.

Look at Canadian content!

Yes, it's one of the silliest things around. Because it seems to imply that we must dig in our backyard. A number of writers are escaping that. Somebody such as Findley will leave that sort of silly stuff completely. There will come a point when the Canadian writer will feel confident enough not even to think about the fact of being or not being Canadian and will write about anything. You don't have the choice. If you live in Canada, if you experience Canada, if you're part of what is happening in Canada, you are a Canadian writer, no matter what you write.

There are parts of my book that will take place in Canada. My character actually ends up in Canada. It seems a very good place for somebody who needs to change his life in an environment where he can choose to be whoever he wants to be.

There are Canadian writers who write about the Second World War, one of the biggest topics for semi-literary or literary expression, especially whodunits or thrillers or political novels. It irks me that some of these writers write about my country, and getting the facts wrong many times. Creating stereotypes, clichés . . .

That is the worst kind of trying to be cosmopolitan. It's when, instead of looking at the rest of the world from wherever it is you are, you dress up like somebody else. It's like the Hollywood school of history where you make a set that will look good to the North American audience, and they don't believe in it. I know exactly the kind of book you're talking about. The writer him or herself doesn't believe in what they're telling. They lack the experience.

I don't believe that in fiction you need to be factually right. There's no obligation for that. What does matter is that you have to feel the stoutness of the man, that has to be true. I don't care if they write about Latin America and they have gauchos waltzing through Guatemala, that is not important—much more important is the fact that if they put within that Guatemalan character a philosophy which couldn't possibly be bred in that kind of character. That is a fictional mistake. It's a mistake of craft, it's not the mistake of a historian or a geographer or whatever. Anybody can make those mistakes, and now you have editors in publishing companies who look up those things and tell you that, "Oh, no, that didn't happen, it didn't happen in 1920, it happened in 1921." So who cares? But the actual sense of who this is, or who this isn't, that is what they do wrong, and that's just bad writing.

In the case of books about Germany, and I will mention for example Sylvia Fraser's *Berlin Solstice*, it is absurd, it is somebody who has learned about Germany by watching Marlene Dietrich films, the Hollywood Germany. It has that absurd sense that everybody was either black or white. The terrible thing is that with the best intentions, intentions of denouncing a certain time or setting moral standards of some sort, they are in fact ridiculing the whole situation. They are making it non-believable.

Like the film, The Longest Day, *where the SS officer is putting the boots on the wrong feet, and the fat sergeant is a buffoon, what with his clanking pots and pans strapped to the horse. This is intellectual dishonesty of the worst kind.*

Exactly. If they were so stupid, then nothing would have happened. It's absurd. Canada is not the only country to make that sort of mistake. For instance in Argentina, because Argentina had never had anything like the seventies. Now writers are writing about it, and some are very good writers, and they write about it as they would write about anything else, with all the ambiguities and contradictions that these stories really have. But others are doing exactly the same and turning it into the Far West, and you have the equivalent of the sheriff and the cowboys and Indians. It never was like that, and had it been like that, it (the war) would have finished in two days.

From the names I have selected for this book I don't think there is one immigrant writer who has specialized in writing thrillers. They all write 'serious' literature. Why?

In a number of those literatures—and I don't know them all, of course—the formula novel is mainly an Anglo-Saxon phenomenon. The French have the *roman noir,* but usually the *roman noir* is much more interesting than just a formula novel. Certainly the Latin American writers are no good at it. I think that if you bring any of your tradition to the country to which you immigrate, many people try to shed as much of that as they can. This is simply not in your tradition. Skvorecky, when he wrote those detective stories—which he wrote before coming to Canada—they are not very good. We are publishing them now because he is a good writer. But I don't know that we are doing him a great service.

If you are going to write formula, at least it has to be good formula. I think they are perhaps not writing it because it's not in their tradition. Literature in most of these countries—outside the Anglo-Saxon world—is not something you make money with. You don't live from literature. It's very difficult to make Canadians understand the immense luxury about somebody like you and me sitting in an office like this and being able to do this sort of thing.

A writer like (Jorge Luis) Borges would still thank almost on his knees somebody who would pay him who would publish him—I mean *The New Yorker* published his stories. You work and then you write, and that's how things are done in most countries in the world. Not that that's good, but I'm saying that Canadians don't realize how fortunate they are that they can do it.

C.D. (Dino) Minni

C.D. Minni, who passed away in the summer of 1989, was born in Bagnoli del Trigno, Molise, Italy, in 1942, and grew up in British Columbia. He was a writer, critic, editor, ghost writer, and translator. His short stories, critical articles, and author interviews have appeared in a number of literary magazines, anthologies, in CanLit textbooks, and on radio. His published works include a collection of short stories, *Other Selves* (Guernica, Montreal, 1985); he also edited an anthology of stories, *Ricordi/Things Remembered* (Guernica, 1989), and co-edited *Writers in Transition* (Guernica, 1989). From 1977 to 1980 he was on the staff of *Canadian Authors & Bookman* as a literary critic, and also reviewed for *The Vancouver Sun* on a regular basis for eight years, until 1984.

He was chairman of the Italian Cultural Centre's Literary Committee in Vancouver from 1985 until his death, and co-ordinated the First National Conference of Italian-Canadian Writers in Vancouver in 1986. He was also West Coast representative of the Association of Italian-Canadian Writers from 1986 until his death.

JURGEN HESSE: At what age did you come to Canada?

C.D. MINNI: Actually I celebrated my ninth birthday on a CPR train somewhere across Saskatchewan. The first week of April and all I remember seeing from the windows was snow. We arrived in Vancouver, and one memory I have is a beautiful spring day. And a girl at the CNR station, selling tulips from a cart. I used that detail in a story.

Did you come from where many Italians here come from? From either Calabria or other regions in the South?

I actually came from Molise which is a mountainous region east of Rome. My father's uncle was actually the first one from Munari village to immigrate to Vancouver. That was in 1913. Some relatives of his came a few years earlier who were homesteading. One of my uncles came in 1924, he was seventeen at the time, and we came after the Second World War. So our ties with Canada go back through relatives for at least the majority of a century.

Is it true, Mr. Minni, that when you go back to Italy, or when people go back to Italy, they refer to both Canada and the United States as America?

Yes. 'America' is a general term. If they want to say Mexico or Brazil they will also refer to it as America. A continent rather than a country, or two continents.

How did you get into writing?

Quite by accident. It goes back to high school when I needed an extra course to graduate. I had to fill it with something. I took a creative writing course, and I enjoyed it. I discovered a talent I didn't know I had and then, being disabled at the time, I thought writing was a good way of keeping up my mind. Physically I had quite a serious disability, but I felt that my mind should not go, and writing was a method of remaining mentally sharp.

Has it worked?

Yes, I think so. I wanted to write a historical novel at one point but the market wasn't there, so I felt I wanted to be a more serious writer, and reading Canadian authors I realized there was a difference between them and me. That I could not write from their point of view. What I had to do was to go back to novels and start writing proper roots and travel forward from there.

At that point I knew no other Italian Canadian who wrote. Years later, when I was to meet them, I realized they had come to the same position as I had. Not only that, but even though we were not aware of each other, we were all basically the same thing. Even using similar metaphors and energy. That is, we were all writing about the immigrant experience, essentially the Canadian immigrant experience, combined with the Italian background. Since the publication of my book, *Other Selves*, I have had letters and compliments from readers of non-Italian background who identify with the immigrant experience because immigration is the common denominator among Canadians. You can also appreciate that in a large country like Canada, immigration occurs not only from without the country but also from within. For example, a Newfoundlander who is working on an oil rig in Alberta is very much an immigrant. A Prairie farmer in Toronto is very much an immigrant. Even sometimes going from a rural area to a city, one is crossing cultural boundaries. This is true for instance of our native Indians when they come into the city. Many agree it is a cultural jump.

Sometimes with disastrous results.

Yes. And there is a pain involved. Not a physical pain—emotional, psychological—and it is these things I wanted to explore in my writing. Also there is a journey back to one's roots which many immigrants feel they have to make. When coming to Canada they have sort of left a part of themselves behind so they feel they have to make a journey back to their roots, and when they do, they discover that the country that they left has changed, and they have changed, and in some respects they are marginal to both cultures. So I wanted to write about that.

Another thing I wanted to explore was the generation gap in an immigrant family which becomes a canyon between the first generation and the children who grow up in Canada. Many of them cross cultural boundaries every day, going to school or to work. At home they are taught one set of values, and in the outside world they have to live by another set of values. It is very difficult on them, especially during the teen years, the years of discovery, of identity crisis. So the search for identity is another thing that I explore in my writing. What else can I tell you?

Ethnic identification is much more of a current trend than it used to be. I came (here) thirty years ago, when immigrants tried as fast as they could to speak English as well as they were able to, and their kids should only speak English, because that was the way of the future. Now a lot of Greeks and Italians and other immigrants are going back to their roots, being rather proud of their background.

Yes, the pendulum has almost swung the other way. When I was a teenager, and we are talking about the sixties here, it was quite common to rebel against one's background. This is an English country, and we have to go the English way. Today, it has become quite chic to be proud of your background, and I think that has something to do with your identity. In a world that is changing very fast, one needs a certain anchor, and one's ethnic background is a form of anchor, an identity. Hey, I am Italian, or I am German, or I am Chinese. So, while things are changing very, very rapidly, according, sometimes, to the imagery projected by Hollywood and other media . . . I wanted to write about that, and I notice, too, that beside being a writer I am also a critic, an Italian-Canadian.

The voices of writers change as they grow older. The change is essentially when children who were rebels in their teens in turn become parents. They get another insight into their parents. I have not written about this so much about myself, but I notice many of the other Italian-Canadian writers have explored this theme.

In my present writing, I am trying to reflect more the Italian experience today, rather than the Italian-Canadian experience of 1950 or 1960. It is a reflection of the community more as it is today, not as it was. It has changed. First of all it has changed socially and economically, and no longer is the Italian of the group a poor immigrant. They have become the third most prosperous (immigrant) group in Canada after the Jews and the Asians. So in that respect it has changed. But their image of themselves has also changed. They come to Canada usually with nothing but a dream, and their dreams have come true. There is a sense of pride in that.

How did they make this dream come true?

Through hard work in every generation, mostly. And by pushing education for the second generation.

Although they themselves may be undereducated, they recognize the value of education?

Yes. (They are) a generation who may have nothing but a grade four or five education. But they recognize the importance of acquiring an education for their children and pushing it, usually financing their children's university tuition, for instance. I think this has something to do with Italian history, where higher education was usually for the wealthy, for those who could afford it. There was a dream the Italian working class had, that in Italy they could not arrive at that goal.

I understand that circumstances are changing there since then, but for those who came in the fifties and sixties their mentality has remained what it was. Their image of Italy has remained one of a poor country. They remember the time after the Second World War. My father, for instance, gets his veteran's pension from the Italian government. And he inquires now, "How can a poor country afford to send a pension overseas?" He doesn't realize that the country is now prosperous, the fifth industrial nation of the world, just surpassing England.

What is your preferred language when you write?

I write in English. I do translate from Italian. I can write in Italian, but I am not quite as fluent as in English. I can't get the same subtleties. Although I think of the Italian that I knew as a child, and I speak it, though now not quite so very perfectly, but I speak it. That influence is in my English prose, and there are, in my writings, a number of Italian words. Sometimes even dialect words.

Yes, I remember some Piemontese (Piemonte is a northwestern Italian province) words were spoken in Torino, where I grew up. Something that interests me—I find that when I return to Germany, my native language has changed. I am totally out of date, and when people speak to me I understand perfectly what they say, but I discover Anglo-Saxon words. Is that the same in Italy?

Yes. Some words, for instance *evergreen*, which in Italian is *sempreverde*, is easier to say in English.

And that came from television?

Television, movies, other means.

The great American dream. The whole world wants to live like Americans, right?

Not necessarily, because it can happen the other way around too. Well, there is *pizza* and many other words that come into English from Italian. So I think of it not so much as an American influence, but of the world becoming a global village. There is more mixed change. There are also more people moving around. There never has been such a large number of people moving around as in the twentieth century. So this relocation, and the alienation that goes with it, I think on a central theme is of the twentieth century, and of the things that I have touched on in my writing from the point of view of the Italian immigrant. But it is a large theme. I think it is one that will touch many people for different reasons.

Do you write nonfiction or do you fictionalize your stories?

My stories probably have a start in reality, but then I transform them into Art with a capital A, so it is definitely fiction. I specialize in short stories. I will some day attempt a novel, but at the moment I am working on another series of stories. I have a background as a literary critic, and so I have read the Italian-Canadian works in particular, and many of the great Canadian writers, and I can see how the two are different. For instance, the English-Canadian writers are doing basically what the Italian-Canadian writers are doing, but they too are exploring their roots.

Margaret Laurence started with *A Bird in the House*, which explored her Scottish Presbyterian Manitoba roots. Rudy Wiebe wrote about his German Mennonite roots, and others write about their Maritime roots. So I think we become a nation of many different writers pursuing a different route, thrown onto the same track, as it were.

In 1985 I approached the Italian Cultural Centre here in Vancouver to begin an annual series of literary events, to give diverse voices a forum and an audience. In 1986 the event was the first National Conference of Italian-Canadian writers. Many of us had not met before, but within the five days of the conference, everyone was friends. We all realized we have something in common. One writer remarked that the villages of the future will not be people all in one place, but people sharing a common interest. During those five days we remained a village. So when I saw them on the last day, sixteen of us formed the Association of Italian-Canadian writers, and that has grown to about forty or forty-two members in three years.

All writing in English, or some in Italian?

In English, in French, and in Italian. One thing I noticed at that conference was that the voice, even an Italian-Canadian voice, is different if it comes from Quebec, from Ontario, or from the West.

Regional differences?

Differences. I noticed with the writers from Quebec, many of them tri-lingual, some of them wrote in all three languages, so in a sense they provide a bridge between what Hugh McLennan called *Two Solitudes.*

There is a group of writers, for instance Romano Perticarini, who lives here in Vancouver, who write only in Italian. Romano—his voice started out as a voice of basically an Italian exile. If you read his later works you can see how that voice had changed from that of an exile to that of an immigrant, that of a Writer with a capital W, appealing to a more universal audience. I think that is probably the route that most every writer will go.

The resistance has come mostly from 'lost writers' who defined the Canadian identity in the sixties largely in a rebellion against Americanism, but (they) defined it according to their terms, not realizing that this image is no longer accurate for the eighties and the nineties. The fabric of Canadian society has changed, and the literature will have to change with it.

Can you give me some examples?

W.O. Mitchell, Alice Munro, who still writes about Ontario in the

1940s and '50s, to some extent Margaret Atwood—all the major English-Canadian writers think that they represent Canada. At the last Vancouver Writer's Festival I went to see Timothy Findley. It was a dramatic reading of one of his short stories which I enjoyed very much, and the master of ceremonies said this was a real immigrant writer. It is us. I was sitting in the audience and I felt 'Hey, I can enjoy him as a great writer, but it's not me.'

I have to be careful not to lose my cool when I encounter traces of xenophobia. The kind of feeling that, 'We English-Canadians are the essence of Canada. You came here, you have to adapt to us.' What happens many times, being from Germany with a heavy past, some well-meaning and fairly intelligent people fall into imitating a Hollywood SS colonel speaking in falsetto. They appear to do this kind of thing with a grin on their face, perhaps not thinking that they may offend. Have you observed this (kind of behavior), either personally or with others?

Not personally. There are ethnic jokes, stereotype Italian jokes, some are made by Italians themselves. I have people call me a *wop*, thinking they are calling me a derogatory name. I say to them, "Hey, we call ourselves that, in pride." So that puts an end to that. My grandfather, one grandfather was actually a *wop*. He was smuggled in from the United States just after the First World War. He worked there on the railroad for seven years, lost the job in 1929. He returned to Italy with his savings.

What does wop *mean?*

It means 'without official papers.' There were a lot of *wops* in the States in the twenties, but the majority were Italian, so the name was given to them. What happened, to give a historical background, is that American unions were clamoring to have immigration restricted because the immigrant would work harder for less wages. It was hard for them to be organized. At the same time the captains of American industry needed workers. So the American government in the twenties put a quota on the number of immigrants allowed into the country. Which satisfied the unions, but at the same time they closed one eye to the flow of illegal immigrants entering the States, which kept industry happy.

It is the same now with the undocumented workers from Mexico. Officially they are not allowed in. But they come over because the captains of industry want them, and they pay them relatively less money. So things haven't really changed.

No. Of course there is revision of that in the States now. Let's face it, Canada and America were broke when they brought some immigrants. If you look at our society today, the most menial jobs are still done by immigrants. Native-born Canadians prefer to stay on UIC than, what can I say, work as a dishwasher, or to pick fruit in valley. It is hard work, and it pays about the same as being on welfare. So they stay on pokey rather than work.

Doesn't it have to do with pride that many immigrants have? The kind of pride that says, 'I will not go on the dole,' as the English say.

Yes, and the fact that they came to Canada to better themselves. You cannot better yourself when you are on welfare. So there is that aspect of it too. I think, too, they have the work ethic, which in North America is slowly dying away.

Romano Perticarini

Romano Perticarini was born in 1934 in a poor but beautiful section of Italian countryside. He came to Canada in 1967. His three published volumes of poetry are *Quelli della Fionda,* or *The Slingshot Kids,* published by Azzi Publishing of Vancouver in 1981; *Il mio quaderno di Novembre,* or, *From My November Record Book,* published by Scala Publishing of Vancouver in 1983; and *Via Diaz,* published by Guernica Editions of Montreal.

Perticarini calls himself a proletarian poet. In a foreword to his *From My November Record Book,* Michele Pirone calls Perticarini "an inspired artist who speaks a universal language free of shackles which would restrict his ideas and blur his imagery." Perticarini cites Pier Paolo Pasolini, the late Italian filmmaker and essayist, as a major influence. He lives in Burnaby, B.C.

JURGEN HESSE: Where are you from, and when did you come to Canada?

ROMANO PERTICARINI: I was born in Fermo in 1934. This is close to the Adriatic Sea. After I was twenty-two or twenty-three years old, I passed from Fermo to Bologna, and in this town I worked for five or six years. After that I came to Canada in 1967.

Did you write in Italy?

Yes, yes. I wrote poetry. I started very young writing poetry. I started in elementary school. My teacher liked the poetry very much and tell me, "Come on! Try and write the poetry!" But, you know, the work stayed in my pocket. Nobody knew.

After I came to Canada, I missed my mother. My mother died in a car accident and in my mind the poetry started again. I really did the first poetry in Canada in 1967 in December, when my mother died. After this, I published the poetry in an Italian newspaper, and I received many telephone calls. Many friends liked the poetry, and I began writing again, not only for myself, but for someone else. If somebody else does not find it interesting, I just do it for me, and that is that. But the minimum I received was twenty calls in 1967, and first of all somebody tell me, "I am sorry for your mother, but I see your poetry is very good." I remember my mother, somebody said she was the same way.

After this, I tried again, I write another three or four more poems. I took this to an Italian newspaper, and then I remember this editor, he tell me, "What are you doing here? This is very good. Why don't you go into a contest? Why don't you read poetry? Why don't you make a book? Why don't you do something with it?" And slowly, I entered Italian contests in poetry.

From here I sent to Italy. And the first time I participated, during a national contest, I won the third prize. I flew home in 1972 and picked up my prize. A gold medal. Yes, this is the Italian poetry contest. In Campodoglio there is a Government House, and I went there to pick it up. I was very happy. Now I continued writing poetry. I like poetry. That is my limit, a short story, for poetry.

In which order were your three books published? This is the first one, Quelli della Fionda, The Slingshot Kids?

This is the first one. The second one is *Il mio quaderno di Novembre,* or *From My November Record Book,* and the third one is *Via Diaz.*

And that one doesn't really translate?

Well, *Via Diaz* looks like "Diaz Street." This is Via Diaz, the street where I was born.

How much has Canada influenced your writing?

This is very hard to explain to you. Now, maybe too much, maybe not. But before I came to Canada my poetry was really only for myself. We are born in a different way and maybe influenced very much more than the influence in Canada. But I think, for me, Canada influenced me very much. A long time ago, my old country, my old house anyway, my family, (influenced me very much). This, I think, moved something to my mind. I don't have a very clear idea of this.

May I suggest that, if you had continued to live in Italy, you still would not be published?

You are right, yes.

Here they accept you more.

Exactly. I have one poem here. Maybe I can find it here. This is the first poetry that I wrote here when I came to Canada when my mother died. This is very important.

Maybe I can read it in English.

Yes. It translates really differently. I have not found a good translator, but it is okay, no problem. This is it here.

It is called Your Cross:
   "Like fields of wheat
   There, erect iron and marble
   Confront me.
   Crosses equanimously divided
   By paths of dark pebbles
   Amidst vast expanse.
   I sought one—yours.
   While flowers
   Withered in my hands.
   And there it was—
   Weathered by time, yet legible:
   'Your dear mother.'
   In my hand, those flowers, wilted,
   Draining fragrance and youth

Secreting droplets
Abating along petals
Like mourning tears.
I promised the wind,
The crosses,
The cold marble . . .
I shall return once again
If there be another tomorrow."
It reads better in Italian, doesn't it? It flows better.

Yes, thank you. It sounds different. *La tua croce.*

"E lì, irte e disteste
come un seminar di grana,
di ferro e marmo le croci
innanzi mi si pararono.
Un viottolo di scuri ciottoli
tante a destra come a sinistra
di ugual parte le dividea.
Una da tanto la cercavo
ed il fiore in mano
lentamente s'appassiva.
La, logora dal tempo
ma ancor vi si leggeva:
'La tua cara Mamma'
in mano il fior reclino
con la sua perla di rugiada,
perse profumo e giovinezza
e come una lacrima
il petalo rigava.
Dissi al vento, alle croci,
ai ceri, ai freddi marmi
di cui ripieno e il loco:
tornero domani,
se un domani vi sara."

Now, this refers to cry(ing). I passed 41st and Renfrew, and I see the cemetery. It is completely different from the cemetery in Europe. In Europe there is marble all over. Over (here), only flat. Closed and flat.

This is a cultural difference. I was raised in Italy, so I speak with my hands and let my emotions out. We shout, and we cry . . .

Yes, really. I remember, I went to Germany for one year exactly. I went to school in Germany for fitter and welder underwater. *Unter Wasser.* In Hamburg, a very top school. A very top shipyard. Over there I feel the same. The people are quite warm, a little bit warm. It is different. In Canada I find it completely different. Not quite too cold, but I don't know—different.

Do you have mostly Italian friends?

All over. Everywhere. In a twenty-four-hour day, twelve hours a day I talk all Italian language. In my house too. My friends speak perfect Italian. In English too. But not for me. My daughter same thing. She is not here. She is thirty years old, and she speaks perfect Italian. All of my friends when in my house speak Italian. Where I work, no. I speak more English. But my English is in technology, as a fabricator. Now if I go talking to a lawyer, I go crazy. He uses a different language, a different language from what I talk every day. I never had time to go to school (to learn English properly). I never had time. My wife, she speak English quite well. She works as a dressmaker and she speaks all the time in English to customers.

What interests me here is L'Eco d'Italia. *Is that a good paper?*

Yes. It is nice.

When you published your poems in L'Eco d'Italia, *somebody encouraged you to go and write and publish a book. If a German-Canadian poet were to write in the German language paper, I don't think the readers would be interested in poetry. The German community is not as tight as the Italian community, so I don't think a German poet would stand a chance of being published here. I may be wrong, but I don't think so.*

I don't think so either. The same problem happens for the Italian too, sometimes. The people read the Italian newspaper. The people like to see the poems in the paper, but it is after you publish a book like that, you invite the people. People come, sometime . . .

You are working on a fourth book?

Now I am working on the fourth. Yes. I have a problem first. I want to know. Carlo is a translator, he is a very good translator. He did a very good job. I take it from little Carlo and sent it to a friend of mine who is more English than I, and everybody looked and said it was good. After a few months I received a grant from the Secretary of State to ready it for publication. But what happens, the publisher sent back to me a proof, and in the meantime phone to me and say "Hey, Romano, I need it back in one week. It goes to press right away." In one week I don't have time to sent it to Carlo to copy (proofread). He is now in Lisbon, Portugal.

I check in the Italian language; everything, correct, not bad. I sent back right away to, and I tell them, "I hope everything is okay in English because I have not seen it." And they say, "Oh, don't you worry about anything. It's okay." Well, first mail refused from Portugal, one letter, I sent to Carlo the copy. After one or two months, I received nothing from Carlo. What happened?

I phoned to him and he tells me, "Romano, believe it or not, this is not my son (his translation). This is a bastard." I said, "What happened?" He told me, "What happened? X changed ninety-five per cent. There is something very bad translated. Something." Okay, fine, no good, no bad, I pass over. But it is not like that. And now I am in trouble. Carlo from here look like my brother, and X doing me a favor for the publication of the book. Now I am from the hammer to the . . . what do you call it in English?

Now it got from bad to worse.

Yes. I received a letter from X to inquire, "Why do you change to . . . ? I don't understand." Now, I believe that Carlo translated my next job and I eliminated X, and I would like to make another book and include a few poems from this, what I like, plus the new poems that I write, and I can make another book, *Boy of Yesterday*. It looks the same from the memory, a little bit different, but just as good. I hope everything comes out okay. Pretty soon. I don't know how long, but I hope like that. I need X to give me back the copyright for the poems. Just a small letter. After this I leave this one like that. I have thrown away many others. I don't like that. I don't like Carlo to be upset much. I would like to write another one pretty soon.

Very good. Is this a good publisher, Guernica? Sort of ethnic publishers?

For me a good publisher. I think English and many others, I think. I don't think it is only Italian. But the trouble with *Guernica*, they want to put their hand in anything. This is no good. If it's for you in your English language, you check your job and it's no problem. In my Italian he never changed anything, but in English the translator changed too many things. This is not fair, especially when somebody puts your name as translated by Carlo, and Carlo is a (publishing house) director. This is not a small name. You can't do it like that. I don't believe it's right like that.

What kinds of publications do you read? Italian or English?

Italian.

So your working language to all intents and purposes is Italian. Are you going to try to write in English?

You know what happened. I need to go to school before I try the first one. I need to go school. For me, it is very important to go to school. In this interview, you know how poor my English language is. I don't like it like that. I remember the presentation of my book in the Robson Square Media Centre, and I talked to everybody in the Italian language. For me it made no problem. Everybody was happy about what I was talking. This is my language. But, for English, I cannot read in it. I need to go to school. This is very important. I hope in September, after coming back from Italy, to go to school.

You are going back to Italy?

Yes, I have a prize in poetry again. In August, yes. In Milano. Lions Club in Milano. I won the second prize three years ago. This year, I don't know. In the finals now. I don't know yet.

How wonderful! I don't think too many writers win awards when they go and leave their country.

I don't know. Sometimes I have a good poem. I will show you this one. This won the second prize in Milano.

(Reads the poem) Yes! I like it. Read me a few lines in Italian, because it is so musical.

(Does so.) A different sort of sound.

Tell me, when do you write?

Oh, any time.

What do you work at now? What is your job?

Welder and fitter. Fabricator.

So you come home, and you still have the energy (to write poetry)?

Yes. Sometime. Sometime (I write) maybe in work. I just remember
something I have seen the day before, or whatever, and I put a note
in my pocket, and when I back home, I think, oh yes, this is a good
job, and I complete it. Make a poem, or whatever. Oh yes, this is my
life. All the time. Sometime it is very funny. I drive, my wife right side
to me, and I say, "Hey, Grace, take a pen and paper." Then I talk and
she writes it.

She believes in your poetry?

Yes. Very much. She believes my poetry is really nice.

*During the breaks at your job, do you ever talk to your Canadian colleagues
about your Italian poetry?*

No.

Why?

Well, I never. I am really quiet.

*Perhaps because your colleagues at work—the other welders and fitters—
don't like poetry?*

No. They don't care. No. If I go as a welder, I am a good welder. I go
for literature, I write good literature. Sometimes poetry gives you a
hard time, sometimes it gives you joy. I know this. I read many other
books over there, from professors. Nowhere is there connection to
humans. Technology good. Yes. Perfect. But this is too cold. An
iceberg.

It is exactly what I think about academic poets.

Yes. This is academic poet. Academic poetry is perfect in a language, but imperfect to communication.

Sentiment. Sentimento.

Exactly. *Sentimenti.* Nothing. You know, a man picks a flower. Just another one, maybe. Here. Look at the few words here (points at a page). The man have communication to the mother—to the friend. "I picked a flower from the ground and give it to you. I did not take a rose or whatever, what the technician is talking about. Just a small flower. A yellow flower. A grass flower." This is poetry.

I follow what you are saying, because . . . . Let me try to put a point on it . . . the sense of family in Italy is very strong.

Exactly.

Over here, you will find families disintegrating. They (the children) move out and so, when the mother dies, they haven't seen her much because for the last ten years she was living in an old people's home. But you grieved for your mother, because . . .

Because you live all together. You answer (to her) when you talk to your mother. The mother says, "Please don't do that . . . . " She is like a root from the tree, the mother. You cut the root from the tree, and the tree is no longer alive. The same here. The family cuts the root when everybody (at the age of) sixteen or seventeen years old go everywhere, and the tree dies. Don't know about anything after.

A good poet, does he have to suffer in order to write good poetry?

Suffering, yes. This is true. Some time you see a kid in the street. This kid cry, and you go over there and talk to him, "Why you cry?" Well, you know, "My mother told me," or whatever. Well, after you are back home, are you really remembering the kid as when you were a kid? You remember your mother at some time hurt you quite a bit, you needed something like that.

You needed a slap on the back.

That's right, a slap on the back. You suffer in this present moment the suffering of why the kid cries. The point is the suffering. The point, I repeat, looked like before, enjoy and suffer.

You can go flat. The flat . . . I don't know what you call it really. Flat. No emotion.

Do many people read poetry in Italy?

Yes, many people. Too many write poetry. Maybe too many, but the movement now at this present moment in Italy, the movement is different. The poetry comes from any men. Not only from the professor or the doctor or the academic guy. It comes from the guy who is going only to elementary school. Maybe in dialect. Especially in dialect. But the poetry in Italy, a thousand thousand people are reading poetry.

It looks like anywhere in the world. Somebody go up, up, up, slowly, slowly, slowly and somebody staying flat, or jump down. You know, maybe make a publication, and after, no publication any more. There is no point. The poetry may be no good, or the poetry may be no more than a contest and no progress and no picture of whatever you are reading, something like that. But in Italy there are really too many poets, too many people.

Here it is too few readers of poetry. Poetry is being taught at the university, and the students read poetry. When they grow older, poetry doesn't sell very well.

In Canada it is more materialist. Now if somebody reads poetry, people like poetry in Canada, I don't know, not very many. But if you are reading a novel, you are reading a pocket book in a small story or whatever, you make money, everybody knows. But this poetry, somebody feeling too materialistic.

Do you make any money with your books?

No. No. Look, this is very funny. We need money from the Secretary of State, but I buy (my books) from Guernica Publishing.

You have to buy your own books?

I show you the receipt. I buy from Guernica two hundred and fifty books, and I pay two thousand dollars.

So then you sell them here?

After my presentation on February 26th when I presented them at

Robson Square, and I sold (books) just this evening. But I pay for renting to the theatre. I pay for refreshment, whatever.

For how much do you sell the book here?

Okay. This is ten dollars for sale.

And you buy it for . . . ?

I buy for close to $8.50.

It is a good thing you are working as a welder and fitter, otherwise you could not afford to write.

I know, I am no businessman. I am very happy, but when am not happy, I will make a change into a translator. But poetry does not make a man (rich), you remember. It is impossible, never.

Eduardo Pinto

Eduardo Bettencourt Pinto was born in Gabela in 1955, in the south of Angola. In 1975, at the age of twenty, he moved to Rhodesia to escape the civil war. A year later he left for Ponta Delgado, in the Azores, where he established himself as a poet, novelist and journalist. He was a co-editor of two literary magazines, *Aresta* and *A Memoria da Agua-Viva,* both sponsored by the local department of education. He was also co-editor of a literary page, *Seixo,* published in the daily newspaper *Correio dos Açores.* Several of his books were published in Portugal, and he is represented in several Portuguese anthologies as well as in a volume called *The Sea Within,* published by the Department for Brazilian and Portuguese Studies at Brown University in the United States. He has done freelance journalism, translations of poetry in Portuguese, English and Spanish, and is currently working on a novel about his childhood and civil war in Angola. He lives in Coquitlam, B.C.

JURGEN HESSE: Can you tell me a little about your background?

EDUARDO PINTO: I was born in Angola in Africa. I left my country in 1975. I left for other countries in Africa and ended up in Portugal, living in Lisbon, then in the Azores where my parents were. I lived in Azores for seven years.

My family comes from a Jewish-French background. They left Paris in the First World War and went to Portugal to the Azores. From that point on, the family has started growing. I came here in 1983, more as a curiosity.

Tell me about the Azores.

There are nine islands sitting in the middle of the Atlantic, between Europe and the United States. Population two hundred seventy thousand.

What did you do in the Azores?

I worked in different positions, cultural things, and I was director of a literary magazine, worked for radio and papers, and I wrote and published books there.

You decided to come over here in 1983?

I met this girl there, and we decided to get married. She was coming to Canada, and we agreed that I should come first to see if I would like it here. It is very difficult because things are so different culturally. The language was the first barrier, and then the society, the values. There weren't the things I used to do, because I was so involved in cultural things. There was a lack of those things in my life when I came here.

The Azores, despite the fact that it is a small place, has contributed to the Portuguese literature a great deal, and the cultural involvement of the intellectuals in the Azores is very great. There is a diversity of artist life there that is probably hard to find some place else. There are ramifications of those activities all over the world, where those people immigrate and contribute.

I have, for example, a friend who is involved in many cultural activities at Brown University in the United States, and so there are all these connections with those Azoreans, to their land and their cultural interests.

We talk about 'roots' here. Are your roots in the Azores?

That is one of the problems that I had to a certain point—my roots. I lost them in 1975 when I left Angola, in Africa. The civil war, the memories—I found myself somewhere in the world without family, without friends. Everything was kind of lost somewhere. So when I went to the Azores in 1976, I had the chance of finding my roots someplace, and that is probably why I got so attached to it—the chance of getting to know very interesting people and getting the opportunity to express myself in a way that I was used to. Like writing.

Canada has been more difficult because it is a very wide country, and the lifestyle does not make things easy for us. I don't know too many people, and what I do is write in my own language, thinking of Portugal and not thinking about where I am. Not only because my work is processed on memory, and the strong memory that I have goes back seven, ten, fifteen, twenty years, even more.

Last week for example, when you called me, I was at work on a piece of text related to more than thirty years ago. It is an old picture of me and my brothers in front of this old house in Africa. This picture is the only memory that goes so deep in me and makes things come alive. It is like a starting point for me to go on and not to forget where I came from and who I am.

You have been here six years now. How would you describe your relationship to Canada?

At the beginning it was very superficial because I had a problem with the language, and what Canada meant to me was just a chance of gathering around my economical needs. But fortunately for me that phase is gone, and now I have a more mature and more concerned view of this country. Where I stand now is to get to know what is happening in the culture and to get involved as much as possible with the artists' life in Canada and to know the country as well, geographically.

You work as a letter-carrier to bring in money to feed yourself. Your literary work, translations, and other things, come after 'work.' Do you see this as a step down from the Azores, or is it just a change?

At the beginning I thought it was a step down because I couldn't find interesting things to do culturally, and I was alone, writing with no incentives. But now, I think all this has given me a chance to develop other interests and get a wider vision of the world. Because in Canada you are so privileged to have so many, and such good, libraries, with a wide variety of translated books, and the access to them is so simple. Probably in Portugal it would be more limited.

On the other hand, I do what I like to do most, which is writing, and getting to know North American writers and poets. I get to translate some of them.

And yet, what you have not done so far is write about Canada, if I interpreted you correctly earlier.

What I am trying to do is to compensate for my lack of work about Canada. In my fictional writing I write about my background. I also do translations. So this is the best way to go, step by step to wider activities towards Canada.

Do you want eventually to write in English?

Yes, that is my main interest—to write in English and to be published here, not really about Canada, but probably about something in Canada. I have never found countries interesting enough for me to write about them. But people! People are so interesting, and they can create such marvelous things, around fiction for example. What interests me is to get to know better the country, the people of this country, the places, and to write about it.

Because of the lack of time, and being so occupied with my job, I haven't had much opportunity to travel extensively in Canada. I know a little bit of British Columbia, but not enough for me to go to any one place, stay for a week or two, create an atmosphere and then write about it. It is an option that I have to take one day if I have the financial support to go to one place and try to develop, probably, a North American atmosphere in a book.

I am fascinated by today's gang wars. This subject has to do a lot with ethnicity because so many of these gangs are from visible minorities. They are often immigrants. Does this interest you?

Actually, when I came to this country and I got to know what is happening every day in our life, I find that violence has acquired such a prime status in society. From what I have seen on TV and in the movies, and from reading some books, I don't find much interesting work about violence. In some cases the violence is connected to the sociology of certain groups. It is not the police. It is not the government, but the society itself and the values it has defended. It goes back to family orientation that has created these kinds of problems. If you are living in a society where you are appreciated not for what you are but for what you have, of course sooner or later you are going to have a society that creates that symbolism.

Which way is the society you come from directed?

My father, when he went to Africa, was sixteen years old. He didn't have a mother. He only had a father and twelve brothers, and he was very poor. The only support was a brother that he had there, who never helped him. So he grew up by himself, educated himself in the jungle. There were occasions where for more than a year he never saw a white face in front of him. He lived with the Africans, and he got from them the experience and interesting values of surviving. Somehow he passed them on to us, his children. We are three.

When I was growing up in my country (Angola), I found that what you are is what counts the most. Your voice. Your sadness or happiness. Your intellect, and what you can give as a gift of being, not a gift of materialistic matters. And that is one of the things I miss the most, especially in a big city like Vancouver, this lack of symbolism.

I think you have the key to the whole thing. Gang warfare may be the fault of where our society is headed. You are saying that other societies stress different values, but here, we live in order to consume?

Exactly. For example, two or three years ago, we got a lot of refugees from Latin America. They came in waves, and some of them came with families. If there is a family where the parents have no education, and they came with two or three kids who went to school, and the parents don't work because they can't communicate, they can't find a job, and they will live on welfare. The kids go to school, start learning, and don't have the money to buy the other stuff that the local people have.

So they find a way of going in gangs and stealing or whatever the gangs do to get the financial means to acquire what they want to have. Because society created the need for them to have these things. If they were living some place else where you wouldn't look good with this Walkman that costs three hundred dollars, or these glasses that are made by Porsche, or something else, then of course you wouldn't have to steal to get those things. And peer pressure is one of the factors that creates this kind of accessibility to gangs and violence.

There is also a lashing out at the symbols of affluence, which takes the form of violence. Can you understand this?

Yes. I have never been to New York, for example, but I know there are areas where just by walking you would probably not feel very good about yourself. I have two friends living in Portugal, and one day they went to New York for a week, visiting. They were walking on a street, and this woman was robbed by three black fellows. My friends could not do anything because the others were very strong men, and they could be beaten up. But anyway the woman was robbed and was left bleeding on the street. This reflects what the government and our society has allowed to happen. Places where people can survive only through violence. Violence in our days is a status.

I have seen kids getting the wrong message, by saying that it is cool to be tough, it is not cool to be good-hearted. If you wear sunglasses on a rainy day, and you put grease on your hair, and you walk as if the world belonged to you, and you don't care about anybody, and you don't say good morning when you go to places, and you don't hold the door for ladies coming in or out, and you treat people as if they were nothing, then you are cool.

It is what the new generations are getting at. If you don't do something about it, this is going to be the society of the future.

If you were to write about this, would you write about the society and its goals, rather than the gangs themselves?

I would. It is hard to know the answers for this kind of problem, because it is a very wide problem that has to touch individual by individual. But we are creating a new man who prefers to sit in front of a TV for ten hours a day and eat chips and drink Pepsi. And not read a good book. And leave the kids around, not having time to teach them, and not having time to know how they grow. So, we abandon the kids. Everybody is so self-centred that the only thing they can see is their toes. Looking down does not open their eyes to reality.

If I were to write a book about the gangs, I think it would be very difficult for me to do it. Because it is more serious and more profound and more complicated than one can imagine. I wouldn't have to write about the violence itself, but from where it comes and where it goes, and the solution which I would try to find, because it would be so complicated that I would not feel I had the capacity to solve it. I think it is something very interesting that would attract me.

Actually, my latest novel is called *The White Passage of Silence*. It was published last year in Lisbon, Portugal. The whole book is an epic story about these people who have chosen to abandon the cities and congregate in a place in the desert and from that point create new values and a new society. The book reviewers in Lisbon called the book very strange. I could not understand the word 'strange.' I could not understand if the theme was so pure that it was strange to their minds, or if their minds were so obscure that they could not get the purity. I liked it very much to have the book called strange because the strangeness there was the happiness of the people and the respect for each other.

So, in writing what is a kind of remedy for an increasingly violent world, they thought, "What is going on here?"

Well, it wouldn't happen. Because what I created was a world where a man could feel fulfilled by only having a cup of coffee and sitting in a chair in the sunshine in front of the ocean. Feeling good about himself. Not having to race from point A to B and come back with his mind and heart empty, and the fulfillment of those people was to be alive and have the ocean and the small pleasures that we should have never gone far from. A man only needs a pad to sleep, bread to eat, and a road to walk. Now we have airplanes, we have cars, we have telephones because we don't want to go any place. We have televisions because we don't like families.

There is a term here . . . . I was talking to a fellow not too long ago, and he was putting the family like a vanished thing of the past, without any interest. And when we come to a point where a family is neglected to the point when it is taken as a kind of disease or a thing of the past, we can't have much hope for the future.

So, you are contrasting the violence and breakdown of the family in the cities here with a more peaceful society where individuals are valued?

I only believe that a man can be happy in his life if he is loved. If a child never gets a kiss or a hug from his parents and kind words every day, he is going to the gangs.

The television is only a symptom of the disruption of family life. How about if I threw other things at you: ambition, competitiveness, power, influence— are those other symptoms?

They are. That is how people fight for those false values. If you have a Mercedes and you drive to this hotel, you have the doorman running to open your door. If you have a Volkswagen Beetle, rusted all over and noisy and park in front of the hotel, the doorman is going to ask you to remove that car because it doesn't fit the atmosphere. So, men are responsible for the degradation to the point where we fight for such emptiness. We are going to end up surrounded by ruins, smoke, and distant voices. Voices we cannot understand because we cannot interpret the cries.

When I have to listen to kids saying, "I don't want to speak your language," when they are talking to their (immigrant) parents, "because your English is ugly and I don't have to learn that because I am now living here," I get very sad, because if a child doesn't want to learn their parents' language, and they are living in this country, they will never be able to go back to their roots.

That is true. Why don't you go back to Portugal and have your books translated into English so we can read them?

I have spent six years here, and I don't know this country well enough to decide if I will stay or if I go. At this point, I am staying. I think it is very important to write according to my memories which are very important to me. It does not matter whether I am here, or whether I am in Portugal, or in Greece, I will have to write about them anyway. The only thing that probably I am missing is the time to do it. You know this country is very big, the lifestyle sometimes is horrible, and socially it is cold. I was born in a tropical climate. Somehow I think without sun, you live without smile. That is why I explain a certain happiness of being, just because of the weather.

The happiness of man is a complicated matter. It is very vast, and I was thinking deeply about it. But I think the happiness throughout the decades and centuries and years have changed according to the world.

I think the way things are, society empty of values and feeling, that has created more unhappiness among men, and the only way to be self-satisfied with the life in the world is to go to a place where you can wake up in the morning and have all the time you want. Look in the mirror, shave, smell the coffee, go outside and do whatever you like, without being worried about watches. I would prefer to break my watch right now.

But you have to be at your postal station at seven in the morning.

Exactly.

What message do you try to get across in your poetry?

There was one day . . . I was in the Azores. It was a very peaceful lifestyle, and a poor friend was trying to be philosophical about life. I told him that my perfect world would be where I could be seated, hearing the birds of silence flying.

One of the greatest things, and more romantic, and more poetical, is the voice of a human being. If you cannot hear that even in the silence and the different vibrations, we are lost. We have too many cars. We have too many radios, Walkmans, and innovations to make people avoid communication. Too many planes. We are coming to a point where even the patience to hear another person talking is gone.

So the time is so short that people don't even have the ability of listening to others. I devote my mind and my peace to things that I enjoy. One of the things I enjoy mostly to write about are feelings, a feeling of serenity and a world with peaceful manners.

People do not have time for serenity, do they?

They don't have time, and if you talk about serenity you are likely to get fired because serenity means time. Time value. You are not giving time value to be yourself. You are given time to perform within eight hours where you should do probably—on serenity time—sixteen hours. So when you go home, you are a different man, because your normal activity destroys your patience, and that goes back to what we spoke of earlier, society. The pressure of work, the pressure of transportation, the false values that we have created. If I have to perform a task within eight hours and run all day, certainly when I go home I have no patience to teach my kids about geography, or poetry, or literature, or their homework, or to sit beside them and talk to them because I am too tired to do it. Or to talk to my wife.

You have children?

My wife is pregnant again. She is Portuguese, from an Azorean family, and she comes from a place where family and the ocean are connected.

Family and the ocean.

They live so together that sometimes I could hear the rumble of the ocean when she speaks. The place is so small that it doesn't matter where you look, you see the sky and the ocean and a bird passing by. These kind of people are different.

Are these also birds of silence passing by?

There are connections there. That is one of the things I miss, though, those old feelings of passing by places where the men gather together, smoking their cigarettes, maybe homemade, without shaving for several days, with their heads tanned. I remember, for example there is one island on which there is a place where in the afternoon the men go. It is a wall which they call the stone of laziness. If you go there, you see this group of men seated. You sit among them, and ten minutes later you say hello.

It's that slow?

It is the lifestyle. And then you talk, because you have all the time in the world to speak. If you walk too fast, someone is going to call you and say, "Why are you walking so fast? The island ends right there."

It sounds as if this is a major theme in your writing?

It is not the state of laziness that attracts me, it is their philosophy. Like one time a friend of mine, who is a poet, went walking to the mountain with a man who knew the island very well. This friend wanted to write some poems from the top, seeing the city at the bottom. They got to this place where they found this lagoon. My friend could just be attracted by the silence he found there, and the call of the waters. Since it was a very hot day, the guide took his shirt off while they were walking, and when they got there, they were looking at the water, and right away the guide put the shirt on. My friend said, "Why are you putting the shirt on? It is so hot still." And the man said, "I can't face the water, it is like diving for me, without my shirt." At first he couldn't understand. Those people live on the small island, their respect for life goes through the first stage, which is silence, so valuable.

I would like to make a jump now. I am tempted to call you a writer in transition. Would that be a fair description?

I don't know. Because probably it will be if I have certain books written, then I will look at myself and see what I am going to write about now. Transition to . . .

To your newer reality here. Because you are still a foreigner, living in a foreign land, it seems to me.

I understand what you are trying to say. I can only write about things I can relate to. If I don't find anything that I can relate to here, I can't write about it. I did have some experience on writing columns to a newspaper in Portugal. I sent over probably thirty articles. All of them were related to daily events of the city here. For a while I knew the people liked the work, but then I saw a dead end there, and I stopped doing that. Because meanwhile I had to write this novel. It was more important to me, and so I stopped. I think I could probably be more connected to the land if I was in a small place where I could smell the different stages of the seasons. Where I could be related with the people and go through background, people with roots in this land, who could teach me how to live here.

I can't be myself among one million people speaking thirty languages around me, and not even noticing me. If I have the attraction to something that makes me feel the need of talking about it, I will write about it and that will be the transition. Otherwise, I will go back. For example, I am working on a small novel now, located in Peru. I have not been in Peru. I met some people from Peru, and now I am doing some research about it. It is going to be a short novel, and I hope to have it written this year.

I have another project that is almost finished; it is about civil war in my country (Angola).

Does it cover the period during which the dictator Salazar died?

Yes. So that gave an opportunity to those countries to be truly independent from Portugal. Unfortunately it was a very badly conducted case of independence, where instead of giving peaceful transitions to those countries, they were given violence and war and poverty. The most unthinkable way of leaving. It (the novella) is set to get to know how superficial and how cruel and how empty our media can be. Talking about South Africa every day and not going to that country and seeing what struggling means. Apartheid is horrible, but I don't think it has any more importance than the civil war in my country.

Comparing the level of living of the South African black man to the blacks in my country is like day and night. At least they have their own universities and schools in South Africa, and they have a chance to live. In my country a man doesn't have a chance to live. He doesn't have a chance to choose. They have to run with their memories, walk thousands and thousands of kilometers to a safe place because they are not given a chance to live. And then, we have the United States on one side, the Russians on the other side, the Cubans on another side—it is so crazy that I cannot understand, and I don't believe we have serious people living in this century—to have such a situation and not to do anything about it.

I can see the time coming where writers are writing for other writers, a few intellectuals, and a few others who are not sold on television. We are a minority already, but we will become the invisible minority. The hack writers in Hollywood will be the intellectuals.

I think our society has got the writers they wanted and because of lack of real interest, the real artist cannot make a living any more, or probably never did. For example, if you want to survive as a good poet, doing a living on writing, you have to write trashy novels. A woman with glasses and makeup can write on the way to work and on the way home.

I am concerned that here is a place of dignity. The arts are of very profound interest to me and a very serious matter. If you cannot survive purely on your beliefs, on your way of expressing yourself, without any pressures, there is no future.

Where will we find the good writers? They will be disappearing. We are going to have violence on television, and a microchip mind. I love computers, and I think they are a great tool for writers, for example, word processors. But I don't like to think that computers will create a man without emotions. I want the computer to be there for us to use it, and to simplify our work, or our world, but not to be servile to it. The other day I had a visitor, and I received him in my office where he saw two computers. He didn't look to the books first, he looked at the computers, and then the first question toward the computers was not what I had the computers for, but if I had games to use with the computers. I said, "No, if you give me games, I won't use them, because this is only here to work for me." But it is one of the contrasts of the ways of the computer age. If you have a computer at home, you buy games, you play it. You stay there ten hours. Nothing exists around you but those games. If you come to the world in a situation like this, then I don't see any advancement.

If you work in an office where you have a postman coming every day, the postman is just a piece that comes and goes. It is like having a typewriter there and a computer and a photocopy machine. When you need a photocopy you go to the photocopy machine, but you don't necessarily look at it. Just go to the photocopier and back. A man walks in with the mail, drops the mail, you say thank you or don't say anything, but you don't notice him. You don't care about him.

These are the things I hate. Because we have to look at the eyes and we have to look at the face and the hair, the hands, the movements, and hear the voice, the tone. The shape of the face and the feelings behind it. If you don't care enough toward the next person, you can't care about it any longer because if I act like this to anybody, I will expect the same. That is what the society is coming to. Automation. If one day I have to go to this island and sit in a chair and see the rock of laziness, I will do it.

Elfreida Read

Elfreida Read was born in Vladivostok, Russia, of Estonian parents in 1920. When she was three, her parents left for Shanghai, China, where a number of relatives had already settled. There she attended a British school and later married a Britisher. During the Second World War she and her family were interned by the Japanese. When the war was over she had her first child, a daughter, Jeani, and in 1947 she and her family immigrated to Canada. Soon after arrival she discovered she had tuberculosis and was confined to a sanatorium for a year, where she first started to write stories for children. A few years later her second child was born, a son, Philip, and soon after that her first book was published. Since then she has published eleven books for children, poems in various literary magazines, a collection of poems for adults based on her China experience, and, in 1989, the first of a three-part autobiographical account of life in China. She lives in Vancouver, B.C.

Her publications include *The Dragon and the Jadestone* (Hutchinson, London, England, 1958 and Engelbert Verlag, Germany, 1971); *The Magic of Light* (Hutchinson, 1963); *The Enchanted Egg* (Hutchinson, 1963, and Lippincott, New York, 1965, as *The Magical Egg*); *The Spell of Chuchuchan* (Hutchinson, 1966, World, New York, 1967); *Magic for Granny* (Burns and

MacEachern, Toronto, 1967); *Twin Rivers* (Burns and MacEachern, 1968); *No One Need Ever Know* (Ginn & Co., Boston); *Brothers by Choice* (Farrar Straus & Giroux, New York, and Doubleday, Toronto, 1974; TV mini-series and movie, 1986); *The Message of the Mask* (Gage, Agincourt, Ont., 1981); *Kirstine and the Villains* (Gage, 1982); *Race Against the Dark* (Gage, 1983); *Growing Up in China* (Oberon Press, Ottawa, 1985); and *A Time of Cicadas* (Oberon Press, 1989).

JURGEN HESSE: What was your life like when you were a child?

ELFREIDA READ: Things were getting really, really tough in Vladivostok. I was three years old, and we travelled down to Shanghai by train and settled there as best we could. We lost everything. My parents were allowed just a little bit of money and some possessions, a few.

Times in China were always turbulent. They really were. The settlement was okay—the International Settlement. And that is where we went, to the International Settlement in Shanghai where we had relatives. For a little while we lived with the relatives and then managed to get on our own. My father got a job with a Swiss firm, but by then he was in his fifties, and it was hard for him to get anything really good. He had had a good job, and we lived well in Vladivostok. It was a terrible shock to them. It was a cultural shock to suddenly find themselves in this totally alien city.

So we were sent to English schools immediately because my father spoke five languages, but he figured that English would probably be the language of the future, and so he made a point of always speaking to us in English. But my mother always spoke to us in Russian because of having lived in Vladivostok in that society. So I grew up with the two languages simultaneously.

I would come and say something in Russian to my mother and then turn to my father and say it in English, almost as though he had not understood what I had said although of course he had. So it was always like that. This went on all through my life in the Orient. I went to Shanghai public school, which was a good school, but totally in English, although we were taught French. We lived there and lived through various Chinese troubles. The Chiang Kai-shek thing.

What was your father doing?

He was an accountant with a Swiss firm. They were a printing concern, but in Vladivostok he had been an import/export person for specialty books. He loved books, and he loved reading. He actually more or less smuggled a whole German encyclopedia into Shanghai. It was in twelve volumes, and he used to translate from the encyclopedia to me whenever I wanted to know anything. He would read it in German and translate it to me. So I grew up with this encyclopedia in the family.

At what age did you leave Shanghai, and where did you go?

We left Shanghai after the (Second World) War. We had been interned by the Japanese. By then I had married my British husband. We were interned, and when the internment was over, when the war ended, we left.

Tell me more about that time.

We were married in 1941, and my husband's parents were in Canada, as well as his brothers. He wanted to get married, and so he stayed on in Shanghai, intending—you see, I was sort of like an enemy national there for a while. Because at that time, if you remember, Russia had a pact with Estonia, and it was on the other side. So he thought we would get married and then we could go to Canada where there wouldn't be any problems.

And then the Japanese came while we were making all these happy plans. The Japanese struck Shanghai on the same morning as Pearl Harbor. You see, it was . . . anyway, they struck and immediately surrounded the International Settlement, and everybody stayed in the settlement and could not go out. Then they started to build the concentration camps.

So we just continued living our lives. My husband was working with the Shanghai Gas Company, and I was working with another concern as a secretary. We just continued working, and the Japanese were preparing the concentration camps. It was scary. But it was okay. And then, a year later, they started to intern people little by little.

So they took you out of the settlement and put you in a concentration camp? What were the conditions in the camp?

The camp we were in was a famous camp. This camp was the same camp as in, I don't know if you saw *The Empire of the Sun?*

No.

Well, don't. It was about this camp, and it was totally untrue. Anyway, we were in this camp. It was a university compound, the Chinese University. The Japanese had attacked in 1937 in Shanghai, and that university had been partially bombed. But there were many buildings left standing, and we were quartered in those buildings. Twelve to a room. I was there with my husband, living in cubicles. It was cold. We were quite hungry, but there was no mistreatment, and we had an excellent commandant who was a very humane person and tried to do his best for us. But it was so scary, wondering what was going to happen, whether things would change. And, of course, as the war progressed and grew worse for the Japanese, our conditions got worse too. We got less food and less care.

So this lasted four years, or until the end of the war?

No, from the beginning of 1943.

Until 1945.

Yes. They (the Japanese) surrendered, and the Americans took over the International Settlement.

How soon did you come to Canada?

After that we left in 1947 and came to Canada in August of 1947.

When did the first urge strike you to write? Can you recall?

I was already writing when I was a very little girl. I used to write little stories and things. Then I went into poetry in my later teens. Actually in the camp we had sort of a little literary group, and we used to write things, stories, poems, whatever. But nothing really serious. Then, when I came here, I found that I had tuberculosis.

That was a serious thing in 1947. They did have antibiotics then, didn't they?

They had just come in. But I didn't go into hospital, I didn't even know I had it, you see. I was just feeling lousy. I thought, "Oh well, it

is a new country, I have had a baby, so of course I must feel tired."
And I had no servants any more, I had to do everything myself. But
then of course I realized that I was just too tired. Every time I sat
down I fell asleep. So, I went into a sanatorium and was separated
from my little girl who was by then three years old. I started writing
stories for her.

Where was the sanatorium?

It was right here, in IDH, the Infectious Diseases Hospital at Vancouver General Hospital. We were there. We had excellent care, and
I was extremely lucky because antibiotics had come in. Not the really
good ones. I was very lucky.

So anyway, I think I felt separated from my girl; I started writing
these stories. But I didn't really do anything with them until . . . .
You see, I came out, and there were five years when I still had to have
treatment. I had pneumo-peritoneum which is when they collapse
your lungs, and I had to have that for about five years. A long time.
To make sure that it had healed.

By then I was in my mid-thirties, and I had my son. I was allowed
to have another child. You were advised not to have a child until you
were recovered. And so everything was kind of upside down at that
point, and I didn't do any writing. But then I looked at the stories
again, later, and finally began to publish the children's stories and
stuck with the children's things.

Looking at your latest book that came out, what is it called?

Time of Cicadas. But this is for adults, this is not a children's book.
This is going into two more sections. This is the first part of a
three-part . . . you will see on the back.

*(Reading) "This is the first of an extended three-volume autobiography to be
known, when complete, as Days of Wonder."*

That I have been doing really for my children. This is real. Autobiography. More or less what I have been telling (you) in the beginning
of this conversation. But this only will go up to the end of my China
years. These three books.

But I always wrote poetry for adults. I have continued writing
that, and I have published quite a lot of it. I have never collected it.

No?

I don't know, the older I get, the poems I wrote earlier don't seem to be that great. So I think, well, maybe some day I will put it all together. But the autobiographical account of China I wrote especially for the kids so they would know more about me when I was young.

I didn't know all that much in regards to my own mother. A fair amount, but not as much as I would like to have known about her. Her real thoughts and feelings, not as much. I suppose that she was very busy coping with immigration and all the disasters. There were so many disasters in Shanghai. There were always wars, always uprisings, you know. Fighting on the streets. It was a hard time, but in between we had fun.

Is writing primarily influenced, in your opinion, by experience, or are there sometimes writers who have a vivid imagination, who use fantasy and acquired knowledge from reading or other media, and then fashion it into books?

Well, in my own case, I think that you really have to experience something for it to come out sounding genuine. I think you really have to live through experiences. Sure, you can have your imagination, or whatever, but I think that is probably why I have never turned to the novel because I just feel that I really have to . . . I like books that are true myself. I like autobiographies, I like travel books, I like poetry because I always feel that good poetry really comes from the heart, and that you really have to go through whatever it is that you are writing.

It doesn't really come through the cerebrum, does it?

No, no. Not the really good portion that stays with you and sort of flashes up in the middle of the night. So I like poetry, and novels are fine. I read a lot of novels. But I always find that suddenly my credibility will kind of snap, and I think, "O well, this could go any way, couldn't it?" So I lose interest. The novel is always in jeopardy when I read it.

In a novel about wartime Germany I saw, on the first two pages, three major errors in fact. I put the book aside; I just could not continue. The author didn't do his research properly. I asked Alberto Manguel about this and he said, "Well, if this is a really good writer, it doesn't matter whether the facts are right or wrong." I differ with him there. What is your opinion?

Yes. I would differ too. Because as soon as I see something that is not right factually . . . . There was a movie that was a book first. My cousin read the book too. She started marking all the places in the book where the author had made factual errors about the city. Streets and the weather. For instance, the weather was all wrong. She began marking them, and after about a third of the book she gave up because there were so many things wrong, it was just impossible to keep up. It's better, in such a case, for an author to use a fictitious background.

Invent a city.

Yes, invent a city and use your imagination, by all means. People who like to read imaginative works will enjoy it. But don't ever mix facts that you are not certain about with imaginative things. It doesn't work. I feel that unless you have experienced this particular incident, or whatever you happen to be describing, it just will not come through as genuine. I really don't think it does. Then it becomes ludicrous.

Do you like writing?

I love writing, but I don't write that much. I write when I get a good idea. I don't force myself to write, ever. And, I suppose, I like to write about ideas more than about anything else. If I have some thoughts about a society problem, or perhaps a religious problem . . . . I have written in my book about *Brothers By Choice*, which was made into a television series. I wrote about a real son and an adopted son, and the problems between the two boys. This is for young teenage people.

The point I am making is that this was a subject close to my heart because, not in our family, but in brother-in-law's family there was an adopted child. There were some problems of one kind or another. So I wrote about that. Then I wrote about a mentally-handicapped boy, which was also a problem that was very interesting to me because we had such a friend. The problems that faced this child were always very close to my heart because my own son befriended him. So that is what I mean, I write more about ideas. I don't know what to call those ideas.

Concepts?

Concepts, societal problems, that kind of thing.

You operate on various levels; on the level of poetry, and then on the level of some phenomena of society such as adoption and mentally-handicapped people. Then, later in life, you arrived at the autobiographical stage. Many people write their autobiographies when they are forty, and what have they really lived through? You did it later in life, and now we have this first volume, and two more will be coming. Your years outside of Canada weren't really dealt with, or not treated by you in books, until now.

That's right. Well, I did do a trilogy for children about Chinese legends. These three books were about a little girl who travelled through China and met the various characters in the Chinese pantheon. Those were my first three books.

You say you don't write much, but by what you are telling me, you have quite a stack of books here!

I think I have published eleven children's books and then these here (pointing to the coffee table), so about a dozen or more.

Do you have a special preference or not for fellow-immigrant writers?

No, I wouldn't say that. I judge by the book. I don't really care who the writer is. Male, female, Russian, English, Chinese, whatever.

Have you thought about the difference between an ethnic writer and an immigrant writer?

No, I have never considered that, really, because I must say I have always thought in English. I have never thought in Russian that I can remember. I must have done when I was little, really little. But I have always thought in English. I went to an English school, I went to an English church, and my family was an immigrant family, but through my school and church connections I was mostly friends with children who also spoke English and were interested in English books and the English sort of thing. Then, of course, I went into the English camp and was with all the Britishers. When we came here I didn't really feel anything. I often wonder what I am. I don't think I am anything at all. I have no identity whatsoever.

Is that frightening to you, sometimes?

No, it is not frightening. I think there is a sort of nostalgic thing sometimes that makes you wish you were a real Russian, or a real Chinese, or a real Japanese, or something. I don't consider Americans real, or Canadians. I am sorry, but really I feel they are a very young nation, a very young culture, and they are not (rooted) in the earth. They haven't got enough of the bones of their ancestors in the earth.

Tender roots.

Yes. Very. It is obvious when the Queen comes here, everybody goes out to see her. Their roots haven't strengthened. But you know, you get roots like people in Germany or Italy. I mean those are really roots, and sometimes maybe there is a sort of feeling of nostalgia, that maybe I would like to have such roots. On the other hand, there is a sort of freedom, too. And you can feel like a world citizen.

You remember all the stateless persons after the Second World War? We heard these stories about a man who was aboard a ship and wasn't allowed to land because he had no nationality. So a stateless writer could be somebody like you. I have changed my country three times, but my German roots are still the strongest. Which of yours are the strongest?

I don't think I have any. I really don't. You see, my father was a very nationalistic Estonian, and he was always very happy during the very brief period when Estonia was liberated. Estonia was liberated for all of twenty years, between the wars. He spoke Estonian. I never learned Estonian. I felt that I was Estonian, certainly, but I never felt any roots, you know, real roots, because they (her parents) were never there. In Russia, I don't remember being there at all. I was three when we came out. In Shanghai, in the International Settlement, I grew up there. I was not Chinese. I was not British, although I was brought up in a British ambience, but I was not British. Then I came here, and I just sort of wonder, what am I? And really, I am stateless, in my heart. I don't have any roots at all, anywhere.

You have a sort of a modified British accent.

Yes. It is a Shanghai accent.

When you started talking about your roots, I would have said, "Well, here is an acquired Anglo-Saxon. Somebody who grew up British and thinks British." But this is not the case, which proves that early experiences are really the most dominant in your life. Otherwise you would identify with the British, would you not?

But why British? I have never even been in Britain.

You know, I love living here. In every respect. But I don't feel it belongs to me, or that I belong to Canada. I am a Canadian, according to my papers, but I sort of look upon it all with wonder, and I think, "What am I doing here?" But here I am. You have a warm regard for a country which took you in and has treated you very kindly in every respect. I have an extremely warm regard for Canada, but I don't really feel I belong here, you know, like a Chinese feels he belongs in China.

I still feel like a German, I have to admit. I have lived in Canada for thirty-one years now, longer than I was living in Germany, or in Italy.

I don't have a mother country or fatherland. In a sense it sort of makes you accept everybody much more easily. You don't have that nationalistic fervor that leads possibly to wars. I don't have that at all. I think that if a writer in Canada is a good writer, that is very nice. If they are British or American or Australian, or Indonesian, or whatever, if they are good writers, and I am enjoying what they have written, it makes no difference to me at all. I don't think you have to make yourself *be* a Canadian writer. I think that it will come about, possibly, if we all stick together, if we don't let this mosaic divide us totally. If we stick together possibly Canadians will finally produce a truly Canadian literature.

When I came in the fifties, that was the major influx of immigrants then, from Europe, and it continued on into the sixties. Now they come from Hong Kong, China, Taiwan, the Caribbean, many of the Third-World countries. There are more Latin Americans coming here, and eventually all this multicultural mosaic, this ethnic texture of Canada, will change again. So where is Canadian literature going to be?

I have no idea.

This is a fascinating aspect, though, to speculate on that.

Yes. It depends on what you want. If you want a Canadian literature, then you really have to insist that everybody speak English. Well, I am not talking about the French-English thing. But the actual English thing. That you educate the children in a certain way. To be more, I don't want to say conformist . . . you just have to have a people who will speak a language well and communicate well in this one language. But if you are going to have a whole bunch of languages and allow it, and encourage it, you are not going to get a true Canadian literature, are you?

When we talk about Canadian literature now, we still talk about Anglo-Saxon-oriented literature. Maybe there is never going to be something called Canadian literature.

And maybe it's not necessary. The question is, do we need it, and is it not more likely that it will come up by itself if it is supposed to come up?

Grow homogeneously.

Yes. Because, really, a Russian doesn't think, "Oh, I must write about Russia, or I must write about Russian customs, or I must have a Russian identity before I can write this book." A Russian doesn't think that. A Canadian seems to think there always has to be a Canadian identity thing in writing.

Doesn't that suggest insecurity to you, a kind of existential angst?

Oh, there's a lot of insecurity in any young country like Canada, or even the United States, which I consider a young country by European standards. I think that is the reason why there is so much violence. It really comes from insecurity, and also it goes into their literature. They are trying to make the literature as exciting as they can, and they are not really looking to writing about their own roots very much. It is like television. The more violence and the more sex you have, for some reason, it is better. Which of course is far from the truth.

Norbert Ruebsaat

Norbert Ruebsaat was born in West Germany in 1946. He immigrated with his parents to Canada in 1952, first to Edmonton, then to the West Kootenay district of British Columbia. He finished high school in Vancouver.

In 1971, he formed Steady State Productions with Brian Shein, and wrote and directed for local Vancouver theatre. In 1974 he began working for CFRO-FM, Vancouver Co-operative Radio, and was instrumental in getting that station on the air, and developing its early broadcast formats. He worked briefly for the CBC, as host and story editor for *Identities,* the ethnic affairs program, and worked as editor and promotions manager for Pulp Press between 1978 and 1985. In 1979 he published a collection of poems, *Cordillera* (Pulp), and since then has been publishing poems, stories and articles in a variety of periodicals. In 1989 his story "Nazis" won *event* magazine's annual creative non-fiction contest, and the Aya Press annual fiction contest.

He has been working for many years with his partner and collaborator Hildegard Westerkamp, creating sound-text pieces for radio and performance. He has also translated a number of stage plays (including scripts by

Brecht, Horvath, Kroetz and Strauss) from German into English on com-
mission from Guy Sprung at the Toronto Free Theatre.

His current projects include *Speaking with Diane Brown,* a collaborative
book on aboriginal-immigrant cross-cultural communication; *Handbook for
Immigrants,* a book of stories and memoirs; *The Father and Son Banquet,* an
ongoing oral history project with his father; and *Poems for Parents,* a collaborative book with his daughter Sonja. He also teaches Communications
at Simon Fraser University and Fraser Valley College. He lives in Vancouver,
B.C.

JURGEN HESSE: Tell me something of your background.

NORBERT RUEBSAAT: I emigrated from Germany in 1952. My father
came over first in 1951, to Edmonton. We came by boat. I remember
it quite well, mainly because my mother was seasick the whole time,
and therefore I had to take care of my younger sister, who was three.
I think we landed in Halifax and then took a train across the country
to Edmonton. From the train trip I remember looking out and
seeing—it was March—snow and endless bush of the Canadian
Shield and thinking that the country is forever, that we were going
somewhere that had no end.

Were you upset about being in this environment?

I was a kid, and I was really excited. I thought we were going to a
magical land. I was upset about a lot of things. It was hard on the
boat, and it was hard being with my mother and my sister and not
having any father around on that trip. When we arrived in Edmonton it was freezing cold. I remember my father coming to the train,
and he had grown a mustache which I had never seen. I thought it
was completely magical to see him at the end of this strange journey.
It was freezing. I had never met weather like that, it was so intense.

Then we lived with an old bachelor, Mr. Currie, across from the
Royal Alex Hospital where my father worked. My father had to do
his exams over again because they didn't accept his (German)
exams, and so he was an intern at the time. He started as an orderly
learning English and making almost no money. My mother then
had to go to work in the hospital as well, and so my sister and I were
on our own. That was very hard, quite traumatic. That memory of

wandering around and not knowing how to speak English and having to take care of my sister.

What happened when you met Canadian boys?

I remember I woke up, as I think of it now, the second or third day in Canada, I looked out of the house and I saw this amazing light that you have in Edmonton in the early spring. It is a very clear northern light (shining) against the houses. I was mesmerized by it. I saw a boy playing across the street, and my conception at the time was that English was a language very much like German, with a few extra words. So I knew a few words, I knew 'yes' and I knew 'hello.' I remember 'yes' specifically. My thought was you just spoke German, and in between you go 'yes, yes, yes, yes,' and that's what talking English was.

I went over to the boy who was kneeling in the sandbox, and I thought, well I'd like to play with this boy and meet my first Canadian. I bent over and kind of sidled up to him, and went 'yes, yes, yes, yes,' and then I started talking. He looked at me as if I was from Mars and moved away. That kind of made me thoughtful. But I tried it again a few times and then he ran away—probably thought I was crazy. And then it started to gradually dawn on me that this might be more complicated. So that is my first memory, and of course the trauma of going to school. I started school in September.

By then you spoke some English?

No, I spoke very little English. At home we spoke German. I remember sitting in school and being incredibly terrified. You just got plunked in and you did the best you could. I was so dislocated and lost, feeling I had lost my country, I had lost my language, lost the world that was familiar to me. I was still excited about being Canadian. But the other image I had of being Canadian was that it was like (being) Indian, and that if you wore Indian costumes you somehow magically would be able to transform yourself into a Canadian and speak the language. I had just basically become fluent in German, being six, I had just incorporated my first language. I thought that you must be able to do it magically because your first language you learn magically, you don't remember how. Suddenly you are thrust into a situation where a whole new language confronts you, and you don't have a conception of what it is. So you want a fairy godmother to touch you and transform you so that you can speak it. I thought it would happen at school. That was one of my fantasies as well. When you are put in school, certainly it would happen because you are in the right place. But of course it didn't happen then either, and there are painful memories of that—of being afraid of school.

Were you ever ridiculed by a Canadian child because you didn't speak English?

There was one thing before I went to school, in the summer, because my parents were working and it didn't work out very well leaving us at home alone. For a while they tried that. They put us in a kindergarten for a while, my sister and me. I remember feeling that nobody could speak my language. I was completely terrified and felt locked in. They would have a rest period after lunch, so during this rest period I would always escape. I remember pushing her (his sister) over the wire wall, and I thought our place was just around the corner, but of course it wasn't. We were in downtown Edmonton. So I walked with my sister around the corner and got completely lost, thinking it was around the next corner, and then it got really freaky because again I couldn't speak to anybody. I kept looking into people's faces to see if there was somebody who would recognize me or whom I would be able to recognize as being able to speak my language.

I remember being called 'German Boy' and 'Nazi' and 'Kraut' because, of course, all of the kids I was growing up with, their fathers had been in the war, and they had quite vivid memories and really hated the Germans.

So after one year, my first year in Edmonton, we moved to Castlegar in the interior of B.C., and by that time I could speak English, although I still couldn't spell or write very well. I found spelling quite hard because you don't pronounce all the letters, and it never made sense to me that you write things that you don't say. Of course I didn't know how to write German either. I did know that there was a relationship between a symbol on a page and a sound, and yet all the diphthongs and the silent letters—a silent 'e' just didn't make any sense. So I was a very bad speller and had very bad handwriting. I fell in love with the girls who had very beautiful handwriting. I thought by hanging around with them I could acquire this power.

Did you ever have to fight?

In Castlegar, yes. It was very organized. We lived outside of Castlegar in a sort of suburb, it was called a subdivision, sort of hacked out of the bush, between Castlegar and Trail. Trail is a smelter town, the biggest smelter in Western Canada, of iron, lead and zinc. All the workers lived in that subdivision. So we were a very strong working-class neighborhood. Mostly Anglo-Saxon and Irish background, although there was a small Doukhobor element and a few kind of diverse Europeans, but we were certainly the only German-speaking people there, or in the area as far as I knew.

We would come home on the school bus and across the railway tracks, which according to folklore ended the school jurisdiction over us, and that's where the fights would happen. And there were fights more or less every day. It was very ritualized. It would be arranged who was going to fight. If a new guy came, he had to fight his way in. But of course I never got in because I was German. I had the double problem of being German on the one hand and my father being a doctor on the other hand. So I got beat up for two reasons. I was never a good fighter. I could never get up the kind of adrenaline where you forget yourself and really go after the guy. I always thought I wanted the guys to like me. I wanted to be nice.

Of course if you were nice in that kind of a context you ended up just being beat on more. So there was a lot of violence. And there was also the traditional hatred of the Doubhobors. The Anglos were hating the Doukhobors. The Doukhobors were generally peaceful, first of all, and they were also much bigger, stronger—they were tough guys. There was very much a pecking order into which you had to fight your way. And, in order to become best friends with so-and-so you had to fight your way through all of these lower ranking people who were in the way. That could shift very quickly. It was all very hard.

There was one point I remember, where I finally did feel accepted. This new guy, this French-Canadian guy, came from

Timmins, Ontario; it was arranged that he would have to fight me. I felt quite honored, in fact, that I was chosen. He was bigger than me, and I thought "Oh, I'm not going to do this!" but at that point I finally got up the gumption to give him a bleeding nose. I remember having this double feeling of feeling terrible, knowing what this guy was up against. Here he was, having to fight his way in and losing, and yet I was feeling very proud, of course, that I had defended the turf and had actually won the fight.

It was postwar. It was very much a war metaphor. The war mentality, and the boys all got beaten at home. It was part of the German tradition my father came from. I went to a reunion in Castlegar in 1984 and ran into my old friend/enemy Gary. He still had that same walk—that sort of a swagger. He asked me, "Rhubarb," that's what they used to call me, "why the hell did we fight so much?" I looked at him and said, "I think it was because our fathers beat us."

What about other races, Sikhs, Japanese, Chinese?

No, there was nobody there from other races. There were Anglos and Doukhobors and Italians in Trail, and some Norwegians and Swedes and a few Eastern Europeans. There was a consciousness that the Japanese had been up in New Denver, which of course is not far away, it's in the Slocan Valley. We would go up there for visits, and we would see the internment camps, some of which were now being used to contain the Doukhobor children who at that time were being forcibly removed from their families and put in a residential school in New Denver. I remember that quite well, because my father got a little bit involved in that. It was also a very hot topic around the Kootenays. The Doukhobors were the lowest on the totem pole in terms of the pecking order, and the Anglos were the highest. The Germans didn't fit in. There weren't many Germans, and no one really knew where to put me except as somebody who was a Nazi, or an ex-enemy. I don't remember meeting other German boys. There was one German family which I met up in Kootenay Lake, in Ainsworth, and that was the only other boy sort of in my general age range of German background that I knew. I felt very cut off, very lonely, because everybody else had a family around, and that was the other thing that we didn't have. We had no extended family whatsoever.

There was no network. Everybody else had networks, aunts and uncles, and it was a small town, a quasi-rural situation, where if the father worked in the smelter they might have a brother working as a logger—they were larger families. I felt very vulnerable in terms of that. The other thing that made me vulnerable was the fact that we were not land owners. Everybody else in that neighborhood, as far as I knew, owned their house, because it was quite cheap to buy. That was a very important part of being a male in that culture. Having your own place and building your own place and knowing what to do and being able to work on your house. All of those things I knew nothing about.

At home you spoke German?

Yes. When we were with our parents we had to speak German. I couldn't imagine not speaking German to my mother. In fact she didn't learn English very quickly although she had school English.

There is a phenomenon I have observed in immigrant families. At home the parents insist on speaking their native language, and the kids understand them but reply in English.

In our family that was strictly forbidden. I very quickly spoke English with my younger sister—I think that happened in the first year. I might be fictionalizing this a little bit, but I can almost remember systemically teaching her English so that I would have somebody to speak the other language with.

Did you like speaking English?

When I went to school, and once I got over the terror of it, I found English very very neat. I really liked it a lot, because it wasn't so harsh and authoritative as German was. It didn't have all this anger in it.

Oh, German has anger in it?

Yes. From my point of view it has.

Your wife is German-born. What is your language around home?

For the first five or six years of our relationship we spoke German. Then at a certain point I found myself getting back into this feeling of being an immigrant, speaking one language at home and another one in the world. Then we switched and tried speaking English. We tried it once and it sounded too weird and didn't work. Then we lived in a communal house with other people and it became practical because the house language was English. That is how we made the transference.

And now?

Now we speak exclusively English, except when we go back to Germany. After about a week or two weeks we will slip back into German. It was very important for me to establish that we speak the language of 'here' not the language of 'over there.'

You were born into the age group that is referred to as the 'baby boomers,' and there was a supposed youth revolution, the phenomenon of—

Phenomenon—there's a good word for it.

Were you part of that?

Oh yes, very strongly. In a way that is interesting because that is also the time when Hilde, my wife, first came over from Germany and we started living together. So in some sense when we started living together I went through a similar thing as I did when we first emigrated. I felt very much a part of Canadian popular oppositional culture and Hilde, being a new immigrant, was quite removed from that. It was quite difficult for her.

Did you at any point reject your German heritage consciously?

I tried to reject it when I was a kid much more. I remember lying awake at nights wishing I wasn't German and especially that I didn't have this weird name. The name was just horrible. I felt it was a weight on me that I would never get rid of.

First or last or both?

Both. Norbert! Who the hell is named Norbert? Nobody is! To me it was a sound that came out of nowhere that was going to curse me for the rest of my life. Ruebsaat was even worse. I would lie awake at night and imagine that I was called Peter, Peter Adams, or Frank Smith. I just wanted a normal name so I could grow up and be a normal person.

Have you ever tried to change your name?

No. That, on the other hand, never occurred to me because I always felt I had to somehow bring that German part with me, and I had to show Canadians that it wasn't all bad, that they could like it.

Of course they didn't really give a shit, did they?

Well, not then, no. Then there was a lot of hate. I found actually during the counter-culture period that you were mentioning—very interesting once ethnicity began to come forward again. That was the first time I dared to feel comfortable bringing in German customs and so on, and feeling that my friends would appreciate them.

Can you give me a year for that?

This would be in 1968 or thereabouts. I was twenty-one or twenty-two. At that time, because the culture here was expanding from this narrow kind of Anglo-Saxonism and actually looking at alternative life styles and so on, having some ethnic background became quite important. So when the '68 counter-culture developed, with one's ethnic background you had elements of lifestyle to contribute that people became interested in, and by that time the anti-German feeling had died down, or at least died down sufficiently that there wasn't this fear of, 'Well, he's German.' A couple of other things fit into this. The first thing is that we moved to Vancouver from Castlegar when I was fifteen. I finished high school at Kitsilano High School, and what I noted there was that although Kitsilano was a working-class school at that time and was supposed to be a rough school, by west-side of Vancouver standards I found it a breeze. I found it totally mild. People called you by your first name, which never happened in Castlegar where they called you by your last name, but you had a monicker like 'Rhubarb.' Nobody ever called me Norbert, except the girls. At the Kitsilano High School there was a much larger ethnic mix. There were a lot of Greek kids. Kitsilano was a mixed neighborhood then, and I felt completely liberated.

And there were Jewish kids which I had never met before. I had no conception whatsoever, and I didn't know what the Holocaust was, or anything. My best friend became Harvey, who was Orthodox Jewish. That friendship was very influential because that made me conscious of my Germanness in a very different way.

In a negative way?

Well, no, because we were best friends, and yet he was brought up with the Holocaust story.

Do you ever feel guilty about being German vis-a-vis the Jews?

Of course. I didn't really find out about the Holocaust until Harvey told me about it. It must have been towards the latter years of high school, and then they showed us pictures at school. I had seen movies, but somehow I didn't associate that directly with them—I didn't have a conception of what it was, because nobody ever talked about it at home. I didn't have a sense that I was personally involved in this. Harvey was the first one who kind of confronted me with that. I had certainly hated being German, or feared being German, because of the bad vibes. Harvey and a number of other Jewish friends questioned the Germanness on a different level and a different kind of guilt came out. I didn't really feel guilty as a kid, I guess I felt not accepted, and I got beat up a lot and I felt hated, but not guilty. Whereas when I became aware of the Holocaust the whole guilt thing came up, although by that time I was quite into assimilating. In my late teens most of my time was spent trying to assimilate.

If you had changed your name to Peter Adams, you could have eradicated the fact that you were German-born. You could pretend that you were Canadian.

There was a secret pride there, however, as well. There was something about what my family called monosyllabic names—Ron Smith—they were not real names. That entered me on some level. At the same time as I thought these polysyllabic names that foreigners have are weird, there was also something about them that made them more interesting. There was something amazing about a name that you had to spend so long saying. There were times when I thought, "Gee, I wish I had that name as a kid." I would imagine myself as a character—usually in books I read. I would read books and the hero would be named 'Chad,' and I would imagine myself as Chad. But it never occurred to me to actually change my name. It would have been a betrayal of my family. It just wasn't part of them.

There was pride. There was a sense that although there was all of this horribleness and hate, there was also something good about being German. That came, for example, at Christmas. As far as I was concerned, we had a much greater time at Christmas than any of the other kids. There were rituals, there were candles on the tree, there was the Advent wreath, there were songs, there were special candies that my grandmother would ship over. There was all this culture that the other kids didn't have. I mean they had a bunch of boxes on Christmas morning and that was about it for Christmas, whereas we had this buildup with songs and the Christmas Story, and that sense of folk culture was very strong and very much a part of my father's way of being in the world. We spent a lot of time, as a family, singing. Especially singing, but also story-telling. So I felt proud.

I think Germans have this strange thing that on the one hand you are kind of hated and oppressed and on the other hand you are superior. Germans have a secret superiority complex, I think even in Europe, and they have always secretly wanted to colonize, as my friend Liliane from Cairo puts it: "The Germans made a big mistake, they didn't want to colonize the rest of the world, they wanted to colonize Europe, and that was where they always went wrong." There is a secret sense of superiority which I certainly inherited and which I struggle with.

Let's go back to the counter-culture. Do you feel today that the counter-culture shaped you, made you into a different person?

Oh yes. I sort of became a hippie first. There was always a kind of parallel, as you know. In the counter-culture there was the drug and groovy scene, and then there was the political scene. I was in the groovy scene a little earlier and got into smoking dope and stuff. But I worked for the student newspaper at UBC and then took a trip to Mexico in 1969. Those two things politicized me quite strongly. I also was hanging around with some friends from school still, and my friend Harvey began to talk to me about Marxism, which I had never heard of. I had no concept of what class was, of the working class versus the bourgeoisie, or any of that terminology whatsoever. So that opened up a new way of looking at things for me. That, along with the sensuous part of the drug culture. Then, going to the Third World, going to Mexico, had a very strong influence on me.

Why would that politicize you, going to Mexico?

Because I saw the clash between the American wealth and the (Mexican) poverty. It was just so striking that I thought, "I cannot live in a world that has these contradictions." And then the Vietnam War was going on, and I could see the same dynamics were happening there. I developed very strong anti-imperialist ideas, and Marxism was also a way for me to resolve the German question, because I began to understand more clearly then why someone like Hitler came along and enmeshed my father and his whole generation in this catastrophe, that then made a good part of my youth miserable. I began to understand it in much broader terms. And then I read Marx and I discovered, not only was he Jewish but also German, and that to me was a great thing because here was this amazing thinker who was from my culture, but also could speak from outside it. I still love reading Marx just for his language.

How would you describe your political stance today?

When I was working at Co-op Radio (the long-time and only co-operative radio station in Canada, supported by grants and listener subscriptions), I was a bit hardline for a while, in terms of my analysis and of the kind of work that I thought I had to do.

Was that the time we worked together? (For a few months in 1976, I was appointed producer of the CBC Radio program Identities, *a weekly hour of short documentaries dealing with immigration and ethnic problems; Norbert Ruebsaat was the host/interviewer.)*

Yes. You probably remember that.

Yes. I remember you being hardline. I found it sometimes difficult to talk to you.

Yes I'm sure it was. I'm sure it wasn't easy for you because I was bigoted in a lot of ways. I think I have changed now in the sense that I am certainly not a new lefty. I don't have any kind of Stalinist leanings. I still believe in dialectical materialism as a way of life and thought, and that will never leave me. But it has become more philosophic.

More philosophically oriented?

Yes. Politically I don't believe any more in the dictatorship of the proletariat or in any of this kind of horseshit. My politics now are very much influenced by environmental thinking. I would say my political sense of self comes out of that. My local involvement is with environment and native issues, and in my personal life.

When were you first interested in trying your hand at writing?

It started with me when I read the Dick and Jane book, when I discovered what a book was, and that I could read one.

What was the bulk of your reading in your young years?

Nature stories, animal stories, and stories about explorers. That was it. Later I got a little bit into sports stories. Lots of stories about Canadian explorers. Mostly adventure stuff. Later still I stopped reading for quite a while. In fact it was connected to that counter-culture period. In my later teens I began to read more about ideas and philosophic stuff. After I graduated from high school, I went to Germany. In high school in my last year I had one very good English teacher, and he was the one who basically convinced me that it would be possible to be a writer. I remember reading romantic poetry with him. I read a poem by Wordsworth, and I thought, "Gee, I would like to be able to do this." It was the first time I had consciously thought that it would be something for me to do.

So poetry was your first love?

Well no, I think my first love was fiction. I had never read poetry before that year. When I went to Germany when I was eighteen, that was when I learned to read German. I stayed there for a year and discovered German literature. That opened another whole world. I started reading Thomas Mann and Kafka and the German masters. That probably was more influencial literarily than any other single source, except the earlier explorer stories.

Does German literature have it over Canadian and American literature?

Well you see, you get into this area of cultural superiority, which is horseshit, you know.

I shouldn't have asked.

To me it is a level of sophistication. There have been no Canadian Kafkas. The closest in English is something like Joyce, perhaps Beckett, and the people who were masters of that generation too. I think literature now is slightly different; we don't have the modern masters in the way we did. I think there is very good writing coming out now. Locally, for example, Stan Persky is a very sophisticated writer. Basically I think there is something to the theory that the war and the Holocaust ended a certain way of writing that will never come back. If you trace Thomas Mann's work you can actually see it.

Didn't the end of the Second World War also open the way for literature in Canada?

That is when Canadian literature started.

Let's look at Canadian literature before we go to your own personal writing. I would like you to try to assess the importance of immigrant writers in this amorphous body of CanLit.

In one sense all English-Canadian literature is, a) colonial, b) immigrant, and I think it works on those axes.

Even W.O. Mitchell, or Margaret Atwood?

Certainly Margaret Atwood, yes. And I think Mitchell too. It is writing that comes to a new place and has to explore a virgin landscape idea—not virgin landscape, but it can't work out of given cultural and geographic conventions.

Why not virgin landscape?

Because the virgin landscape idea excludes the fact that the native people have been living here for thousands of years. I also don't like the underlying sexist notions of the idea of a virgin landscape. So it is this combination of colonial immigrant and in the various kinds of approaches that come out of that—the pioneer approach, the frontiersman kind of approach, the homesteader approach—which is what W.O. Mitchell's tradition is. The basis of prairie writing and homesteading and farming and trying to establish a farm where, one generation ago, there was buffalo. I mean the literature of this land much more directly concerns the actualities and recent history, and the poets are the strongest. When I began writing seriously I started with poetry, and I still think that the early burgeoning of Canadian writing has to do with poetry, not prose, because only poetry can explore those kinds of elemental relationships between geography and language that are really important in order for a literature to be true.

You mentioned immigrant writers as a classification that includes the English-Canadians, or the Anglo-Saxons.

I come increasingly from the native perspective where all of us are Europeans: I mean you (Europeans) have been here eight generations, who cares. We (native Indians) have been here for five hundred generations. So let's put it in that perspective.

Most people don't see it that way. They begin the history of Canada with the advent of Simon Fraser, or Champlain, or whoever.

Yes, with the advent of the English language onto the continent. But this excludes the fact that English is another language. There were a lot of languages before English, and they are still around. If you listen hard, you can develop an ear for those languages, and it is an act of silencing as a writer not to listen to those, and to presume that English is a native language. It is not a native language. It is an immigrant language.

Now there are fine gradations between being a colonialist coming over here, or an immigrant. I think the two conceptions kind of blend into each other at a certain point. I think English people are immigrants in the same way that we Germans are. I think there is an—I almost want to use the words 'official culture' here. It happens in English in that it has been fostered by federal institutions, cultural institutions and so on. I think it is a real mistake for ethnically English-speaking people to consider themselves 'native' as opposed to being immigrant. It is shoddy thinking. I take seriously the issue that we are a multi-cultural nation. If we are going to be a nation we are going to make it on that. We are a multicultural nation that has a strong aboriginal component to it that has to be addressed. That, to me, is a fundamental Canadian political question.

Isn't it being addressed more and more?

Well, it's being addressed on a political agenda, but the fact is that Canada has no substance, no being as a country, because the aboriginal question has not been resolved. Especially here in B.C. We do not have a right to stand in this place and say, "I am from here," because we have not legally gotten this land. You can pretend you are an English-Canadian writer and creating a fantastic literature all you want. Those voices from the ground are still going to come up and whisper to you and say, 'You don't belong here, man. You haven't dealt with this.'

That is something I feel as an immigrant writer in the more traditional sense than you are talking about—a consciousness of language differences and of cultural disparities. I feel somewhere that I can address that in a way that someone who has grown up exclusively in one language perhaps cannot, doesn't perhaps quite see it. When I speak to my Haida friends, for example, I have a real sense of kinship with them. Not on the level of any romantic notions. I have the sense of sharing with them a long cultural history that is different, but having a sense of tradition that reaches back much longer than two hundred, three hundred years, that can reach back into the middle ages and can think in those kinds of time spans. That says I come, too, originally from a hunting and gathering culture, or I come, too, from a culture that was tribal at one point.

There is a bridge linking your Germanic ethnic identity with those of the native Indians here?

Yes. I am just starting to explore that. My next project is to explore that very point. I have just received some money from the Canada Council to do a book with Diane Brown, who is a Haida from Skidegate, to explore this whole question of shared-ethnicity immigrant versus aboriginal. It is a collaborative project.

You started to write at the age of nineteen?

My thinking about writing started when I came back from Germany. During my years of high school I was into sports, and science. I wanted to be a biologist.

What changed your mind?

Going to Germany. I discovered that there was not only natural landscape but also cultural landscape. I discovered a world where everything you saw had been formed by human hands, as opposed to being unformed or where the forming that I grew up with was so grotesque and the boundary between what was civilization and what was wilderness was so abrupt.

It was either houses or bush?

And I went to the bush. Because most of what I saw in terms of houses was ugly. In Germany there is no bush, but there is this whole landscape that has a history and that is shaped and has somehow been touched. I knew that I learned things about architecture—I had no conception of architecture. I learned the history of architecture and how that relates to literature. I began seriously learning about classical music, and I was reading philosophy and mythology. It opened up a different kind of world for me. I think it had a lot to do with coming to read a language (German) that I had spoken all my life. It was like this door opening again. Suddenly this language that I had always heard at home and had tried to shed as I tried to assimilate and become Canadian, opened up in a different way. I became aware that there was more to German culture than the stories that my father told me, and the horrible things I heard about what the Nazis had done. That there was something behind that curtain.

So when I came back, I enrolled in liberal arts first and then in the German department. Part of that had to do with the cultural thing, and part of it had to do with the fact that they offered me the possibility of graduate school and some employment. There was a possibility of exploring German Literature. I went into a double major of German and English. And I decided that I was going to write.

In what language?

Oh, in English.

There was never a possibility that you would write in German?

My concern was that the things about German culture I am interested in and think are important and valuable somehow be made available in English—explained in English. Be translated into English. No, I don't think I would ever master German enough to be able to write in it. You would have to be a genius. You have to grow up with a language in order to write it, I think. Unless you are Samuel Beckett and you could somehow translate that. My concern is very much to translate the sensibility of German into the English language, to give the English language that richness. When I write now, that's what my stories are about.

We haven't had many writers of German origin in Canada.

No, there are not many people writing in that tradition here in Canada, so I guess that is what is becoming my job. I do a lot of translations as well. I have translated five plays from German into English for the Toronto Free Theatre.

Is that easy for you to do?

Yes. Right now I have just finished translating a music theatre piece. I think secretly my identity is as a translator. I am inspired by what the other author wrote, inspired by the spirit of it to translate it into English and to make it available to English-speaking people who are my peers and contemporaries.

'Look how beautiful this is!' That is my basic feeling behind it and why I want to do it. 'Look at the sensibility, and here is something you understand!' I think ultimately it is showing those boys with whom I fought that there is something beautiful about being German.

Do you think they care, here in Canada?

Well, yes, I think they do. I mean there are all kinds of anxieties about Germans but, you know, the Germans are coming back now. So they are going to have to deal with them. What happened in Germany in the Thirties and in the war is not only about Germany.

If German reunification goes ahead—there are stories about Germany every day in the newspapers now. There is a huge ethnic population here which is going to start raising its voice. There is no way that the German question is not going to touch Canada.

There is also this sort of secret superiority which we are going to have to deal with. It's going to take right-wing formations. It will take Stalinist formations. Some of the Germans I know who went through the counter-culture became the worst kind of Stalinists, with the same kind of jackboot rigor with which the right-wingers operate. That is all coming back. So it is not a matter of whether Canadians—you can use the word 'Canadians,' I think, in the sense of a person whose—

Anglo-Canadians?

You have to talk about Anglos. You have to talk about immigrants from Great Britain, and I think you have to be very specific about whom you mean when you say Canadians. I think Canada as a sovereign country is an electoral fraud. The aboriginal question hasn't been settled, and the ethnic question hasn't been settled, and the French-English question hasn't been settled.

The recognition of the multi-ethnicity: Is that what you are talking about? That it is all right to be an ethnic Canadian, which means other than Anglo?

That for me is where the complication comes in. I think Anglos are also ethnic.

Well, you may think so. But the Anglos don't.

Yes, well, then the only other way to describe them is as colonialists.

I don't think they want to do that; there is a stigmatism.

Of course they don't. That means facing the fact that the Germans may have their history, but the British Empire also has its history of oppression and genocide and cultural imperialism and all those things.

Well sure, but they don't see that. Wasn't Hitler a wonderfully evil man, the quintessential monster?

Oh yes, it is very easy to pin it all on the monster. But the German question is going to be on the political agenda, the world's political agenda, for the next ten to twenty years. There is no way around that. It's the largest ethnic group in Europe. It is the most well organized, the most industrialized. It has a strong culture. There is no way you can avoid that, and we in Canada are going to need to know about it. I am not saying this out of any sense of this superiority thing, I am saying it out of a sense of recognizing. We are here as Europeans. The British people who are ethnically British are also Europeans.

I think this question of exploring ethnicity—I am going to use that word rather than roots, because I think roots has become problematical because of (Alex) Haley—has to do with the relationship in your own ancestry to a tradition that connects you to a place, i.e. a landscape, a language, and a community. I always think there is a body, a place and a name. We all have to explore that.

Are you disturbed by the likes of Doug Collins, who don't want so-called coloured immigrants in Canada? Are you disturbed by the new buttons that are being printed in Alberta as we talk, that promote racism?

Yes. I am extremely disturbed by the idea. There is something very important here—this secret superiority thing—if you can turn that around and see pride in it and not fear of your ethnicity. Not pride in any overbearing sense, which of course the Germans have tragically misunderstood, but a real sense of pride in where you come from.

Now we are getting Asian and Third World immigrants, which is on the agenda of the white supremacists. Where is it going to lead us?

I think racism has to be confronted by the people who feel it. I think what is going to happen is that the Anglo-Saxon British tradition has to start examining its own racism in the context of Canadian history and in the context of the history of the British Empire. That is where it has to start. I come back to this recognition of one's own ethnicity. The only way that you can feel as an equal with someone who speaks an incomprehensible language, eats incomprehensible food, and has incomprehensible marital customs is to understand where, in yourself, things become incomprehensible. And there is a point I think in all of us where we also become incomprehensible to ourselves, and that is where we have got to start examining (racism). And that is certainly where I like to work with my writing—at which point do I become incomprehensible. Do you follow what I am trying to say here?

Not quite.

At which point do *I* speak the funny language? At which point do *I* have funny customs? In *whose* eyes do I wear funny clothes? In *whose* nose do I smell weird? So my response to any efforts on the part of that official mainstream culture to establish itself as the sovereign culture of Canada is to say, "You are weird, and here's where you're weird." My response is to turn it around and say, "Look, here is where you become weird as well." And again, not weird in the negative sense, but weird in the sense of different but interesting. I am really sincerely interested in how other cultures solve the problems that we, as human beings, share.

What do we call immigrant writers who were born into the English-language culture?

I have inherited English as the result of colonial accidents of various kinds and colonial intentions of various kinds and I write in it. I love the language. I am well aware that it is also the language that has operated as an instrument of oppression in my country, and that is the edge on which I work with the language. Pablo Neruda has an interesting poem about that, a poem about the Spanish language which influenced me a lot, about the beauty and the horror of the Spanish language as it both oppressed and garlanded Latin America. In Latin America the beautiful Spanish language also silenced the other languages. So there is that edge. The history of the British Commonwealth and the whole history of European colonialism is the only way to get at this whole question and to understand that, as a Canadian writer, I feel a direct affinity with someone like Derek Walcott, for example. What are some of the South African writers? People who are writing English out of a history of British Colonialism. The university departments call them Commonwealth Literature in order to keep it away from the English Department.

Will Canadian Literature be fundamentally changed in the coming years by the writings of these immigrant writers whose first language was not English?

I think it will be. That has a lot to do with the cultural politics in Canada now, through free trade, embarking on a continentalist path again, and that has a lot of consequences for the kind of writing we are going to be able to do. The English departments at the same time are colonized right now by the first wave of CanLit writers and critics and theoreticians.

We are writers in English who come from other cultures. I think we have a lot to give, I think we have a lot to contribute, and there is no way that Canada will save itself as a cultural entity separate from the U.S. unless it begins to take seriously that issue. Otherwise we just become a melting pot. We just blend right into the larger American culture marketplace. I think it is writers from other cultures writing in English who are going to save Canadian literature. I don't see where else it is going to come from. I don't think it will come only from there, but it is a major thrust. I have to bring in the native writers as well. That is an important contribution and an important stream that has to be also included.

Anna
Sandor

Anna Sandor was born in 1949 in Budapest, Hungary. Following the Hungarian Revolution, she and her family escaped and immigrated to Canada. She completed public school and high school in Toronto and graduated in drama and English from the University of Windsor. Following an acting career during which she appeared with the Shaw Festival, Théatre Passe Muraille, Factory Theatre Lab, Manitoba Theatre Centre, and many others, she switched careers and became a screenwriter. Her vast body of work has ranged from the very successful Canadian sitcom, *King of Kensington,* to the highly acclaimed television movies, *Charlie Grant's War, The Marriage Bed,* and *Two Men.*

Her other credits include the television movies, *Tarzan in Manhattan, Mama's Going to Buy You a Mockingbird, A Population of One,* and the feature films, *The Stone Angel,* and *Martha, Ruth and Edie.* She has written for the following television series: *Seeing Things, Danger Bay, For the Record, Hangin' In,* and *Flappers.*

The winner of numerous Canadian and international awards for her writing, Ms. Sandor is married to writer/producer William Gough. They have one daughter, Rachel, and live in Los Angeles.

JURGEN HESSE: Tell me who you are and what brought you to Canada.

ANNA SANDOR: My name was actually Anna Koves when I came to
Canada which is the name I used in a script for my main character.
It was my stepfather's name, and when he died I went back to my
own name. I was eight years old and was brought here by my mother.
What brought us was the revolution, actually '57. We tried to get out,
but we kept getting caught over and over again.

Do you remember any of this?

Yes, quite vividly. There are two things in terms of writing that are
crucial to everything I write about. One is, my father died when I was
five, in fifty-four. Then the revolution itself, the whole frightening
aspects of it. The Russians burned down our apartment building,
and everyone took refuge in the basement. In Europe basements are
pretty secure. The Russians set the building on fire. On the ground
floor was a department store. The Russians wanted to loot the store
so they set the building on fire. We had to flee from the basement.
We had to run across the street in crossfire, and people were
dropping left and right. We climbed out a window, crossed the street
to a building in another street, but they wouldn't let us in because
their basement was crowded. So we had to go back into the basement of the burning building because we couldn't stay out on the
street.

　　　When we tried escaping, my stepfather went ahead of us. My
mother and I decided to go. The first time everyone else in our party
got caught, but we didn't. We just came back to Budapest. The
second time we got caught (trying to cross the border into Austria).
The third time we got caught, and each time my mother bribed her
way out.

Did you come from a wealthy family?

No, we were upper-middle class. We weren't wealthy but well off.
Then we finally got out with false papers. The papers were real but
the information on them was false. We had some doctor friends, and
they signed some documents saying I had epilepsy, which I didn't,
and that I needed treatment in Vienna and after treatment would
return. Once we got to Vienna we got political asylum.

　　　A lot of the things that happened at that time were really

ingrained in my mind because I was eight years old by 1957. It is a very formative age. It was so frightening and traumatic. Also the fact of leaving everything, just walking out. For an adult it's bad enough, but for a child, when you have an idea of your world being in one place, and you walk away—you want to walk away, I could hardly wait to get out.

Yesterday when we were cleaning out the garage (in preparation for moving to Los Angeles) I found a plastic doll, a toy that I had with me all through that time. I remember sitting in a hotel room in Vienna and playing with it, putting Nivea creme on it and taking it off. It was a bad time, but I was glad that I went through it all because it makes you mature beyond your years which, in a way, is good and gives you a lot of material to draw on.

Any war experience, or revolution, tends to sharpen your instinct for survival and burns itself into your memory. Because of these experiences, do you consider yourself possibly a better writer than if you had been born into tranquil, peaceful and serene Canada?

For sure. I often say to myself when I see the writing of younger writers or beginning writers, very often it's third-hand experience emotionally. I haven't experienced everything I write about, but I've gone through a lot of the emotions that I write about. And if you're born into tranquillity and peace, and never having your life threatened, well, I think that everyone goes through incredible traumas in their life. You're very lucky or unlucky if it's all smooth sailing. You're then probably a very boring individual. The actual, physical, life-threatening experience is something that, if you haven't gone through, there's no imaginative process that can take you through it.

It does several things to you. One is that relative to that everything becomes not unimportant, but on a scale of what is important and what is not, it quickly tells you—to use a cliché—there is a bottom line. As I was packing in the garage yesterday I came upon a box of old compositions that I did in school. They were funny in retrospect, but if you think about it, well, there's a story about the Santa Claus parade in Toronto. The story was about a little girl who gets swept away in the crowd. And Santa Claus is described as a sort of ogre. And then the adulation towards this mystic figure!

I was a child when I was writing it. When I was a child the things I wrote about always had to do with death and destruction. It does mature you and does gives you an insight into life which can be warped. Sometimes it does become a little too black. It really helps you look at things from the outside and gives you a perspective on life and death.

I submit that you couldn't have written (the CBC Television film) Charlie Grant's War *if you hadn't had that experience.*

Certainly not. When you read (the CBC Television script) *Two Men*, it's a smaller story, but the emotional scale is as large in terms of the events. No, even some of the things that don't deal directly with war and things of that kind, I don't think I could have written either without my experience.

Can you tell me what brought you to writing?

I came to writing totally accidentally, as a profession. I've always written, enjoyed writing in school and high school. I used to run stories through my head, calling them night dreams as opposed to day dreams. I would have continuous stories going on all the time, for months and months, with dialogue. I always thought the way writers think but didn't realize that. I had decided early on in life, when I was three years old, when I went to see *The Nutcracker* in Budapest on Christmas Day—I was enchanted—I thought, "This is it, this is magic," and I decided then and there that I wanted to go on stage. Since ballet was the only thing I had seen I thought, "O.K., I'll be a ballerina."

As I got older I decided I would become an actress, that was always what I wanted to do. What I didn't realize was that my thinking was more that of a writer. I was too analytical in many respects. I held back too much in my emotions. In writing it's between you and the paper, it can come out, but you don't have to be there.

So I became an actress, and I acted from the time I was a child, and went to theatre, and acted professionally for five years. Louis Del Grande, who had directed me in a play at *Théatre Passe Muraille* asked me totally out of the blue to write something for *King of Kensington*. He'd seen some poems I had written.

How old were you then?

I was about twenty-five. I had gone to the University of Windsor Theatre School, so I had a BA with a major in drama and a minor in English. I don't think you can learn to be a writer. As an actress writing for the screen, well, it really helps to be an actress. I can look at a script and can see what the actor is going through. When one asks something that is impossible for an actor to do, when writers don't know about acting they put things on paper that will not work. So I wrote this thing for *King of Kensington*, and they kept asking me to write more and more, and about a year later I was turning down auditions, and I thought, "I think I've become a writer."

It's a terrible story for people who are struggling to be writers, to say that I accidentally became a writer. When I look back, I succeeded immediately as a writer. As an actress I worked, but it was always a struggle.

There are two groups of immigrant writers. One is very keen and sensitive toward their background and write about it; the other seems to shed this dark past and become totally Canadian in their outlook.

No matter how much you deny the fact that you come from the outside, it will always be there in your writing even if you don't write about it. There will be a tone, a judgmental tone, the tone of the outsider, whether it's the tone of, "I know better, because . . . . "

To say it cannot be part of your writing would be the same as saying that having brown eyes, or being six feet tall, is not part of who you are. It's very much part of who you are. If a person feels insecure because he is short, he may never write about being short, but it will be part of his writing. It's very much the same with the immigrant experience. If you choose overtly to deny it, there must be some reason for that, and I think that reason will be there in your writing. It depends on what kind of writing you are doing.

If you are writing historical, political treatises, that's one thing, but if you're writing fiction, you're always dealing with emotions, with motivations. There are also some people who are professional outsiders, that's all they ever write about, deal with, and I think that's wrong as well, because there are other topics in life.

It depends what you are writing about. With somebody like Elie Wiesel writing about the Holocaust, it took him many years to deal with that, but it is his primary topic. I think it's so huge a topic that he can write about for the rest of his life and not exhaust it. However, if someone comes from Hungary, as I do, and all they ever write about is coming from Hungary, I think there comes a point when you can say, "What else is there? Enough!"

The Second World War seems an inexhaustible topic. There are people who have never been inside Germany, don't speak German, and yet presume to know how the circumstances were.

It depends on what the story is. Years ago I wrote a story that is now dated, called *Running Man,* because of AIDS. It was about a closet homosexual school teacher who was married and loved his wife. At the time, nine or ten years ago, it was a unique story, and it hadn't been done ten or twenty times. It was quite controversial. A now defunct gay paper sent someone to my apartment and asked me the same question, "How can you, a woman, not a gay woman, write about a man who was gay. What gives you the right?" I said, "But that would be like saying Tennessee Williams can only write about gay males in the South. Why shouldn't he write about a straight New Yorker. I feel I have the emotional entrées as to the feelings of this man trying to hide things."

I said I had done research and talked to people. By the time the article came out they were not attacking me, they were not condoning, but they understood. I still feel to this day I was quite justified in writing the story, and that I did a good job by approaching it from the inside.

It's the writer who should be the judge, not someone from the outside. I have turned down writing jobs, people coming to me and asking me to write about the Jamaican experience in Canada, and I said I really know very little about that world. I did not feel comfortable, I felt I could not approach it from the inside. It's something so alien to me. But I know a number of writers who live in urban centres who are familiar with the native (Indian) experience.

When you came to Canada, Canadian literature was not known as a major force. There were a few English and French Canadian writers, and then the immigrants came, and especially the postwar immigration boom. Has Canadian literature become an amalgam of immigrants and native-born Canadian writers?

It has become an amalgam. To compare it with something more mundane, or a lower level than literature, I remember when the first outdoor café opened up in Toronto . . . it was the Jack & Jill, they went into a house and converted it to a coffee house. Some friends of ours did that. I remember once saying, "This is insane, who's going to go into their house and sit outside in the summer? This isn't Budapest." Now cafés are so much a part of every major city. I think it's the same thing with the immigrant influence. Suddenly this whole group of people riding on a wave of blood and war and revolution and discrimination came into a country and started writing about their experience, started exchanging views and ideas with native writers, started dealing with topics which up till then had not been dealt with in this country, looked at things differently. Of course it influences even the people who have never set foot outside of this country.

It suddenly opens doors that weren't open before, even the fact that, yes, people do buy this and are interested, reviewers will review it, magazines will publish the poems—it just opens up. Also it's just the fact that in the last thirty years a lot of wonderful Canadian writers have come along whereas there was just a tiny handful before that time. There is a blossoming. It's the same thing as ignoring steroids for a long time. All of a sudden somebody is breaking records.

What's happened is that the human spirit—whether physically or emotionally—has been shown a new vista, and something has opened up.

That's not to say that Margaret Atwood wouldn't be Margaret Atwood if George Jonas were on the scene—of course.

She is writing about the Canada that has been transformed into something different from what it was through the immigrant experience. In that sense, she is influenced by the likes of you and me.

Yes. This is very true. It's a good mix. It's the outdoor café of the literary mind.

Has Canada become a cosmopolitan country because of the immigrant experience and, if so, might it have had a different, more narrow development without us?

I think so. If you look at what has happened in the last thirty years in the arts and in architecture, and if you look before that for the relatively arid period that went on for much longer . . .

But in those days Europe was booming, Vienna and Paris and Berlin . . .

Even the most rabid xenophobe would have to admit to that.

Now the major immigration is from Third World countries, and our literature has been reflecting this fact almost immediately. What are we looking forward to here?

Certainly there is going to be an influx of something new and very different. I don't think the change will be quite as dramatic as it was (in the last thirty years), because these people are already coming into a very rich picture, whereas, when we first came, it was not as rich. It will probably not be as dramatic an impact. The painting is already very colorful, and they are going to add their own colors, whereas when we came it was beige, shall we say (laughs). Thirty years from now when we are old and grey and in our wheelchairs in the Old Artists Home discussing the past, I don't think it will be quite as cut and dried.

You write fiction, but you write films and serial television.

Primarily television movies.

Can you make a living from that?

Yes, a very good living.

Has the novel as a form ever interested you?

I tend to think very much—even though what I write is very dialogue-oriented, I don't write action pieces—in terms of movies, of pictures on the screen. Perhaps one day I will write a novel, but it's not what I do the best. I find it much more difficult than to write prose. It's a different art form.

I noticed with some dismay that you're leaving Canada and living in Los Angeles because that's where the market is. Is that right?

Yes. What there is in L.A.—the possibilities are limitless. There is a huge talent pool. Here you find yourself as a writer saying things like, "It will be wonderful to get somebody like Dustin Hoffman for this role," whereas there it's, "We'll see whether Dustin Hoffman is interested and available." It's a film-making town. There is film history on every site. I love movies and found it rather inspiring. There is also an incredible amount of air-time on television. In Canada, if you get five television movies done a year on CBC, it's a good year.

From one writer?

No, in total. In 1988 I had three movies on CBC out of five or six that were on. In L.A. they do as many television movies in a week as we do in a year. There is this hunger for product, and the competition, on the other hand, is much fiercer. We're not going because we can't get work here. We turned down more than a lot of writers get offered in a year.

I love Canada, having come from somewhere else. I'm sure you have heard this song before. I love it with a passion. It's the most wonderful country in the world. The one thing I don't like about it is the level of non-enthusiasm. The people are afraid of putting themselves out on a limb and say what *you* say, that you love my work. You so rarely hear that, and it's not that I want my ego stroked, I don't need that. But I think if someone whose work is not fixing telephones or stoves—where there is a palpable result of what you've done—my work is an extension of me—the only way I get a kind of feedback and satisfaction other than the monetary satisfaction, is to have people say I liked it, or I hated it. What you get here so often is, "I saw your movie." (Laughs)

A typical Anglo-Saxon response. They say it was different or it was interesting.

Someone said to me once, "Be careful (in L.A.), because they'll kill you with love." People will say to you without fear of being fools, "I've read your script, and I love it." It really is very exciting. What has stopped for me here at this moment, the excitement has stopped: What will the next phone call bring? You need this to rev yourself up. When it becomes just a job, then you're not doing a good job anymore with the kind of thing we're doing.

I can see this lack of enthusiastic response as a hindrance in the development of a writer who is less self-assured than you are.

Yes. There aren't too many opportunities to fail here. I think we all need opportunities to fail. Because there is so little product, particularly in films and television. I feel sorry for someone who is starting out in films and television. In literature it's different. There are enough small presses that a person can break in.

Are you a nationalist?

I am a nationalist to a certain extent. I am not a nationalist to the extent that everything you write about has to have the Canadian lights flashing on and off. I remember when I first started writing for television, for *King of Kensington,* the only sitcom popular and well-known. I would always get asked in interviews, "What makes this Canadian?" It's like sitcoms coming from L.A. or New York, there's nothing different.

And I would say, "Every single person concerned with this show is a Canadian, it's shot in Canada and aired on the CBC, so how can you ask me what makes this Canadian? What makes it not Canadian? What else could it be but Canadian? Do you think they're going around in the U.S. saying what makes *I Love Lucy* American? It just is."

I am a nationalist in that sense. But I am not a nationalist in the sense that everything you write has to have Canada stamped all over it. What translates, what is understood and universal to everyone is something very particular. If Isaac Bashevi Singer can write about his little village and yet win the Nobel Prize, writing in Yiddish at that, well, somehow it becomes universal. If something is truly Canadian it's Canadian and also universal. I'm a nationalist more in the negative sense. By that I mean I think it's wrong to try and project beyond what you are to appeal to other countries.

I walked away from a country with absolutely no regrets. To me a country, a house, is a place of where you are, but there is always the feeling that you may have to leave it at any moment. It can't become too rooted.

May I suggest then that you are not leaving Canada but stepping out for some time?

Yes. To get back to the beginning of this interview, I don't think of myself as a Canadian. If I had to choose, I think of myself more as a Hungarian than as a Canadian. But I don't think of myself as just a Hungarian or just a Canadian, I think of myself as a mixture of influences. Even if it turns out that we will spend the next twenty years in the United States, I will not think of myself as an American either. The baggage you carry with you has labels on it. Being Hungarian and being Jewish, I can't say that I'm a Canadian.

The first time I went back to Hungary to visit—I was afraid to go back for a long time. I had these nightmares: I went back, and they locked the borders and wouldn't let me out again. The first time I went back I was twenty-one, and I was in Vienna, hadn't planned to go to Hungary at all, and I got a visa and went back. I was really astonished. I was totally at home, and yet I was a foreigner. That's impossible to explain to someone who hasn't gone through that.

Karl
Sandor

Karl Sandor was born in 1931 in Budapest, Hungary. He married in 1954. He learned a trade, then, when he had to, joined the army. He left the army and Hungary in 1956. In 1957 he arrived in Edmonton, in 1959 in Vancouver. He writes in English only, and translates Hungarian poets whom he likes, including Fay and Pilinsky. He writes short fiction and poetry; he is currently working on a volume of poetry.

His works have been broadcast by the CBC, including "Fingers . . . fingers" on *Anthology*; "Vimas" on *Artist in Isolation*; "Harvey" and "Message to the Architect of the Revolution" on *The Hornby Collection*; "Inside" (a radio play) on *The Hornby Collection*, as well as the radio play, "Signs of Life"; "Requiem for a Violin," a special documentary, and "A Poetic Reflection," on *Arts National*; and "North," a documentary, on *State of the Arts*.

His fiction and poetry have appeared in a number of periodicals, including *Canadian Fiction Magazine, Byte,* and *Prism International.* He lives in Vancouver, B.C.

JURGEN HESSE: I think we should begin with you telling me who you are and what your background is.

KARL SANDOR: I came to Canada in 1957 from England where I spent more than four months after I left the country. I was a lieutenant, a radio technician lieutenant in the Hungarian Army, and I had been transferred to the capital to a wonderful new job that would have been a great technical challenge to me, and I was looking forward very much to that new challenge when the revolution came. It was a revolution, not an uprising, in my opinion. That doesn't matter.

And I would tell you, you will be able to reflect on the importance of radio because it was on the radio when I heard that all the officers should report to the closest headquarters, military headquarters. The closest military headquarters where I lived was the Killion Barracks which became a headquarters of the 1956 revolution. You see, I lived in the 9 District, the famous 9 District. I reported there and was introduced to Karl Molita who was a military leader of the 1956 revolution.

I had obeyed the law. They called me in and as a good man, and a good soldier, I went and reported. We had the legal government, and I became the officer of the new legal government, which became very illegal in two weeks. I was a signal officer on a R7 radio mobile unit of the Hungarian Revolution without breaking a law.

Of course it was extremely chaotic. I remember very well some historical figures from that era whom I just met that very day when I went. I took an oath to support the new Hungarian Constitution and that I would obey the rules of the new government. Everything was totally legitimate. In my naiveté I thought that (my country) would be able to convert to an independent Hungary. Boggles the mind, still! It boggles the mind! How beautiful it would have been!

Well, you know, I did my best. There was no independent Hungary in the cards, as we found out. I was crushed by this. I was so naive. Being an officer (who) got a very total Marxist education—with all this, I thought that it was possible. We didn't want to be capitalists again. Anyway, so I was twenty-five years old in 1956, and I said "wow!" this will benefit the masses, this is what I learned. No, there was nothing possible of course. It crushed me so much, it was such a blow, people being shot up, you know, people being butchered inside apartment buildings with machine guns.

I slept in my own little room with my wife and a sub-machine gun under my bed, and there was shooting. I looked out from the outside corridor of the building where we lived, and I looked into a 60 millimetre mounted cannon barrel on the street. I lived inside the house, when I looked out, it was aimed right at my door.

I mean, just a minute, it was such an incredible blow that I never, I am not sure whether I would ever recover from this.

Does this experience have any bearing on your life today?

Yes. Absolutely.

You cannot . . . .

Just recently I have been published in *Prism International,* the University of British Columbia literary magazine here. Probably you are familiar with Prince Igor. Prince Igor is a story, you know, an opera, and Prince Igor declares war on the khan. This khan was one hundred forty miles from south of Moscow. And you know, they go and have this beautiful song, (Sandor sings with great passion). Fine, that's right. Now this Konchakovna is the daughter of the khan. The khan beat Prince Igor's army severely, and they capture young Prince Igor. Now, she sees the prisoners coming into their settlement, and she sings, "Come you old, tired, tired, beat prisoners. Don't be so hopeless. Come and have some fresh drink, some cool drinks. Alcoholic quaff," she says, "and some good food and talk to our young women and forget your worries."

How beautiful the spirit of this. Yet what I learned of the Russians in 1956 was all terrible. Nothing personal, but terrible, okay? I never could understand how come that one side is so beautiful and another side is so brutal, over an oppressive régime.

Are you a Marxist today?

No, I am not! I worked on classics very hard the last thirty years, and I have found that I am without religion and without sides in politics. I would say that if you force me to admit a side, I certainly wouldn't be left of centre. I could tell you, but no matter what color evil would bear, green or red or yellow or purple, it doesn't matter to me, frankly.

Anyway, so let's say, 1956 I came. I wasn't sure whether my being the signal officer of the barracks would bear (me) well, and I left the country, I attempted to leave the country, with my wife . . .

A signal officer of the which?

Of both armies. I was first lieutenant in the Red Army. And then when the communiqué came over the radio that all officers should report, I did. At the headquarters of the revolution I became (an) officer of the revolution, and I had my little identification card, signed by Molita. Molita was (later), of course, executed by the Russians. You know, I met him, I shook hands, and he welcomed me. It was an ordinary thing (this revolution). Regular, not illegal, everything was on the level.

You mentioned your wife.

Anyway, I was a year-and-a-half married at that time. And we wanted to leave the country. We went to the border, and after a day-and-a-half without knowing which way to go—because I never have been familiar with that side of the country—with whatever money we had left. I had been very good on track and field and got some prizes, good pay, and all those things, you see. And I gave it to a guy, a young guy who said he would lead us to the border that following night.

Well, I tell you, the prohibition of alcohol selling ceased that day, so they were allowed to drink alcohol again. He got very drunk. We were out all night and ended up a kilometre deeper in the country than where we started. However, two days later, Russian heavy artillery and tank units were digging in. We were about eleven kilometres from the Austrian border. The irony of (it) all! I had been indestructible, I had been on the Hungarian Army championship team on swimming, running, and shooting. I was special, I thought. Yet it was a cripple, Josef, who was in charge of the calves. They had a separate little manger. Thus, we hid. I took all my rankings off and everything.

And he led us through the border. But before that we were captured by a Soviet patrol, put into a jail, my wife and me, (and) interrogated by three Soviet officers and two Hungarians without a rank. They told us they would put us into boxcars and ship us out. Me and my wife were the only two who escaped from that confinement, from the railway station. They took us to the railway station, we were under guards, and in five minutes I investigated all the windows, all the doors on the railway station.

There was one window that was not guarded. We climbed

through and walked immediately to the Russians disembarking heavy equipment, armed vehicles. Since I knew a little Russian, I asked for matches. We behaved so innocently, we were like locals, and walked right by the railway tracks. I asked my wife, "My God, don't look back. Which way should we go?" There was some small arms fire coming from the direction of the border.

She said, "Let's go the way where the small arm fire (is) coming (from), because there is the border." That kind of a wife I have. She knew, that wife, my yes, that's Margaret. Our life would be in danger, but there is a hope for something better beyond the small arms fire. Anyway, they came to look for us with reflectors mounted on these armed vehicles, but we buried ourselves in the first furrow of the deeply ploughed field. They couldn't find us.

Then we got into this manger where Josef the cripple was, and he helped us through. The first foreigner when I walked through the border was a young Englishman. He was twenty. He washed the feet of my wife. Our feet were bleeding from the hike in ankle-deep water and because the shoes were of very poor quality. It was a pretty rugged passage.

Tell me about fear.

I had no fear. The Russians interrogated my wife, and I had to stay outside the tent for three hours in the freezing weather. My boots were full of water. I had no fear whatsoever.

How do you explain that?

I had committed myself. I rather would have died. I went through hard times under the revolution. I saw innocent people shot up, I took in my arms young people who had been caught in this armed revolution, legs dangling on the cartilages. Took them to hospital, on my back, five blocks from the hospital. I made up my mind. This country, the way it is, I cannot live here. They lied to me from 1945 till 1956. I was the pet of the political science department in the officers' school, I loved it, and I still enjoy it. I don't mind an intellectual debate.

The most potent experience of my life was living in the Second World War as a spectator. I submit that my subsequent life has been molded and defined by these experiences.

I agree. Let me add to this. I was born in 1931, so I was from twelve to fourteen years old when the brunt of the war passed over us. I will never forget the lining up for bread. Three of my uncles died in the war, my favorite (uncle) used to hold me close to his chest, and he smelled of good brown bread, this masculine smell. They disappeared. A train (had) been blown up in Russia. This wonderful part of my family (had) been blown away somewhere. I will never forget when the bombing raids came, this is a major impression in my life, and I will not be able to undo this.

We had a small bunker, maybe a foot-and-a-half earth on the top of these two-by-sixes, and the night bombing. It was wintertime, the ground was frozen. On a frozen ground the impact of the bombs is much stronger than in the summertime, and the bombs hit everything in sight. I lived in a suburb of Budapest. Three houses from us was a forty-foot crater. The bombs fell like this (Sandor makes a series of noises imitating falling bombs in a crescendo) until you half passed out just from the noise and the vibration. So I thought of it as a giant running, and I would hear his footsteps, as a kid, and with his next one he would squash me.

But I was not afraid. I tell you why. I was so crushed that we could not have a country, (an) independent country.

I left the country. Six days later I was in London, England. I wanted to read the newspaper. I wanted to say something about my terrible disillusionment. But disillusionment is too mild a word. It was a tragedy for me. I lost a language, it blew my mind. I had learned German for five years. I learned Russian for three years. And I ended up (in London) on account of that I was such a naive young man. I believed that it is possible to make an independent Hungary. Can you imagine?

I wanted to tell somebody what happened to a dream, and I am still at it. My focus, of course, has changed. I don't talk about the oppressive régime in surrealist or realist modes. No, I talk of even a greater universal theme, man's cruelty against another, especially when it happens in the name of religion. My present work is concentrated on a theme, masses of people being intoxicated by not facing up to the fact that it depends on them what they will achieve in life. They put their faith into something greater, and in the name of that faith unnameable cruelties will be dealt out to innocent people.

When you came to Canada, did you come straight to Vancouver?

No, I was two years in Edmonton.

The events in Hungary changed you. When you came to Canada, did anything else happen to change you?

For the first two years there was a tremendous clash of cultures. I got into some brawls. I never raised my hands first. I looked very innocent, and I had a mild complexion. I was very strong. I have been on my guard for twenty-five years, only in the last five years I have cooled down.

The people, the customs are different. If there was some disagreement here they started to push each other. If it happened where I grew up, when you have been pushed, immediately you have been hit for it. They talk dirty. For me, I thought they were very aggressive. There was a lot of adjusting to do, which I did. But that left some big bruises behind.

Did you ever want to leave Canada?

I put a big distance between me and the place of my birth. I love my new language. I am even intoxicated by it, but I don't possess it well enough. I will never possess it well enough. But on account of that wonderful experience with English, I speak immaculate Hungarian now. I see the old language through the filter of the new. English, for a long time I saw it through the filter of Hungarian, for the first ten years. But eventually this filter had to be discarded. The new language took over, with its own simplicities. Hungarian wasn't pliable enough.

Tell me when you began writing.

I began in 1968 in Canada. In 1973 I had four or five short stories and some poetry. I had to show this to somebody. I wanted to talk about the worries that tormented me. About man in exile, about man who had to leave his tongue and facing difficulties, not national difficulties, but cosmic difficulties. The sky is tremendous over Canada. I mean we can fit Hungary nine times into British Columbia. Immense space. In my innocence, in my naiveté when the revolution came in 1956, nothing lost. So I walked into the old CBC headquarters on Bute Street, and they were moving at the time, and they said, "You clean this (manuscript) up, come back, we don't handle it now. Come back three-four months, we will be in the Vancouver Hotel." I said fine.

Four months later, in a corridor there was a desk and I saw a young man, very nice chap, I found. I told him, "My name is Karl Sandor. I am a Hungarian, and I write." He said, "What do you mean, you write?" So I said, "I write English. You want to take a look at this? I think somebody should do something about it." He said, "Good, Sandor, leave it here. Give me your phone number, I give you a call."

Now, I gave him three stories. He took two. The next six months, I gave five stories to the drama department in Toronto. They took three. Now this was a beginning. The name of this chap was Don Mowatt, whom I have met a number of times after. He took more things. Thanks to my boldness, this rabid naiveté that I have, I go after it regardless of the titles of people. I will go and talk to them. Invariably, they are wonderful. I hope it's not my eyebrows. Somewhere along the line, they would listen. Then I leave the work with them, and the work will do the rest. All I want is attention, fifty seconds, and so I could leave the pieces in good hands.

What is your writing today? How has it evolved? Where are you going with it?

I will read you a very short poem about a writer in exile who writes in his new tongue, yet he is rooted in somewhere else. The title is *Patria*.

>Once he tasted the honey of your tongue,
>He became addicted to it in indescribable sweetness.
>It made him giddy and confused his calculus of odds.
>Now, in exile, like a thief in the night,
>"He returns with a drunken proboscis
>"To tap your sacred sap
>"To read the old poets of his mother tongue."

It is undeniable that he possesses the new language, but it's also undeniable that he has the megavitamins of the old tongue. I will not read this because it is longer than you want. The title is *Alligator*, and I wrote it from the alligator's point of view.

The alligator will open his eyes and see this very beautiful naked young girl coming out of the water. And this girl will lie down beside the alligator and pour hot scent onto his sandwich. But he is mesmerized by her beauty. He did not eat for seven days. He is paralyzed by her beauty. She will put a branch of tree between his teeth and guide him up, it's a big alligator, guide him up the bank. And the alligator thinks, "Oh, yes, this is my territory. I could thrash her, delimb her, dismember her in seconds. I could get back into the water in five seconds. Invulnerable." So he follows. On the way, she looks into his eyes, left and right and left. She says to him, "Oh, what a beauty in your eyes." And the alligator doesn't know. Does she mean him, or her reflection? Then the girl will step on his head, on her way back to the blanket. He thinks, "Should I turn back? Would she dress up?" And he turns slowly back and sees her loading her father's rifle.

What a story!

Here it is. This is where I am now.

You mentioned having doubts. Isn't it the mark of any writer aspiring to be a great writer, to live with doubts all his life?

You almost made me say that one's life passes in continuous preparation to die. I am so full of life, I love life so much I don't think of death. At this point I am convinced that the god I have been taught does not exist. I see so much cruelty against innocent people, children, but these gods don't work out for me. I think it's up to man to better his lot and build a more tolerant society. I had to invent god because I wanted to live by greater standards than those by which I was living.

Every Thursday I meet (with) a small company of writers, professors, poets and other no-goods, and we try to solve the riddle of what the purpose of life is. We never seem to drink enough to find the key. Sober we cannot manage. We work under a bad omen. Several people who used to come there committed suicide or died of accidents and things.

We don't criticize each other's works between meetings. We

became very tolerant now. This is just good companionship of very intelligent men except me.

Don't be so self-deprecating.

Let me be modest, this is the only time I am modest. I tell you what happened to me as a writer the last five years. I wrote about four plays in two-and-a-half to three years, yes, and I started to write prose, and always another novel. I wrote a novel, a very big novel. It didn't get published. I started to write poetry two years ago. Some of them have been published by literary magazines in Canada. I discovered that it is very difficult now to write prose, that poetry became the way to communicate for me. It pressed itself into its essential.

Aren't you excluding a lot of readers when you write poetry?

That's why I went to radio. Because the radio had such an incredible import . . . significance in my life. I go to the radio because I want to tell the people what happens. So I didn't even send material to literary publishers for a very long time.

What do the English-Canadian writers write about in a country where problems seem minute compared to the problems in the countries you and I came from?

It doesn't concern me. I am so busy with my own material. Of course I am reading them but I have so many things to say. I would not be able to reflect, only in a conversation as we have now, but when I talk to people whom I know and care for, I tell them that after Louis Riel, Canadians don't have a hero. They don't have people who sacrifice themselves for a greater good.

Martyrs.

Exactly the word I was looking for. They don't have martyrs, they don't have nucleuses where rabid innocence could collect and worship and take their lumps but push their cause a little further.

Do Canadians have passion?

Yes they have passion. Great passion. I find great passion in French Quebec. I like Michel Tremblay a lot. And Clarke Blaise and a couple of others. I read them. But outside of this very small group, I have been very disappointed. I am talking about fiction, about tapping into the psyche of the country. And there I'm not too excited. There are a few journals in which you are able to read these people. One of them is the *Canadian Fiction Magazine.* From time to time you will find exciting new short fiction. But most often these people will disappear.

It is hard for a new writer to find a man as patient and incredibly talented as is Don Mowatt who would bother with a newcomer like me. There are newcomers from Norway, from the Philippines, from Japan, from Britain, from everywhere, who would be under the onslaught of new experience. I wrote a play, a very far-out play with a universal dilemma, and the members of the jury put a beak on, so they look like chickens. I presented this play and got a letter back from the head of this theatre in Vancouver, New Play Centre, and she wrote that it was unlikely that I would ever find an audience in this country.

I thought, "That's too bad, because I've been concerned that I live in a small provincial town, which I never accept. This was a small provincial town before I moved into it, then it became a cosmopolitan town, it became a big city, because I am in it."

Too bad. I've been proven right. The play they turned down was done, very well, later by somebody else, by CBC Radio.

I read the Hungarian literature, which I'm not impressed with. I've been very impressed by the Canadian-Hungarian literature. I translated some of the works that will come out now at the University of Manitoba. I will have some of my short stories and translations that I worked on with George Payerle. Ferencz Fay died two years ago, but I think in the last fifteen years he was the greatest Hungarian poet, and he lived in Canada.

Are we immigrant writers ever going to feel at home, or are we going to be strangers in this country?

No, sir, the immigrant writers, if the gods will be kind, will make him understand that there are no borders anymore between us. We live on the planet, and we are a creature of this planet, and it belongs to us. If you want to focus your attention on your poem, you could put this into Irkutsk, into Manhattan, or into Newcastle, or München. It doesn't matter. The man will fall in love, the man will die, the man will be cheated—man or woman, I hate to play with this gender, and I'm innocent—she will be cheated, she will be double-crossed, she will do great things, she will find gods, she will lose gods, no matter where on this planet. So borders don't matter.

It's not that Canada adopted me. I adopted Canada. Canada became my country, and I hope they never will try to take it away from me. I will resist it. I have the old Diefenbaker Bill of Rights pinned on the wall in my basement.

Jim
Wong-Chu

Born in Hong Kong in 1949, Jim Wong-Chu was brought to Canada in 1953 as a "paper son," and raised in B.C. by aunts and uncles. By the time he was nineteen, he was part of the Chinese-Canadian café landscape, having worked as a dishwasher-potato peeler, waiter, short order cook, and delivery boy in restaurants and greasy spoons throughout Chinese North America. Eventually he began to put down roots in Vancouver's Chinatown, an experience that has become central to much of his work. After four years at Vancouver Art School, he produced a major photographic essay entitled *Pender Street East*. He has since worked as community organizer, historian, and radio broadcaster, and is a founding member of the Asian Canadian Writers Workshop—as well as being a fulltime letter carrier for Canada Post. His poetry has appeared in a number of periodicals and in the anthology *East of Main: An Anthology of Poems from East Vancouver* (Pulp, 1989). A volume of his work, *Chinatown Ghosts*, was published by Pulp Press in 1986. He is currently working on an anthology of Chinese-Canadian writing. He lives in Vancouver, B.C.

JURGEN HESSE: Would you tell me something about your background?

JIM WONG-CHU: I was born in Hong Kong in 1949. I always had this

184

feeling that I was never ready for this world. It was at the end of the war, and the British had reoccupied Hong Kong. My father was doing fairly well in pharmaceuticals. He was a self-taught pharmacist, and at that time a bottle of penicillin would buy you a whole building. I was told all this quite a long time later, because this was my real father, and my parents actually had a chance to talk to me.

At the same time as I was born, the eldest sister of my father was making plans to escape from China because the Communists had taken over. She would face a difficult time. Also, she had to rejoin the family. By the time she actually escaped and took refuge in Hong Kong, she was well into her late forties, a very strong individual, both physically and mentally.

She was supposed to bring out her first grandchild at that time. The child died during the passage. They would travel during the night and sleep during the day to reach Hong Kong. There happened to be an (identity) paper left over (of the dead child). I was quite close to that age. So, as far as I understand, when she came to Hong Kong they felt they shouldn't waste this paper.

From 1923 to 1947 there was a Chinese exclusion law which prohibited any Chinese from coming into Canada, and during that period probably about fifty people actually had access—mostly diplomats, merchants, or missionaries. After the fifties, the Diefenbaker government instituted an amnesty program, taking into consideration that most records were lost during the war in China.

A lot of people made affidavits to say that their name was such and such, and that they had a son. They would create a son on paper, which is then accorded to a nephew, and this poor guy will have to assume an identity. It was like living a borrowed life.

So you are a paper son.

Yes, I became a paper son at the age of four-and-a-half years. I was taken away from my family. I was quite cognizant of what was going on. My aunt took me to another part of the city to be with her so I could get used to the idea of calling her mom. Of course, I went along with it, as long as it was fun. Then we went to immigration.

In 1952, or around there, I was brought onto this ship and the ship started to move. Then I realized something was seriously wrong. I started to cry. In the ship's hold there were many women in bunk beds, like one huge compartment. Some of the women would come out and talk to me, because I would be crying for my mom.

They would say, "What are you crying about, your mom is right here"?

Yes. And, "This is not your mom, is it?" Some of the other women just said, "Hush, mind your own business." So, I arrived in San Francisco on a President Lines steamship and then went north by train across the border to Vancouver. In due time I started forgetting about my family in Hong Kong.

By the time I was six years old, this woman *was* my mom. Unfortunately, we had a lot of problems because she was a village woman, essentially uneducated. She did not know how to take care of me. We lived in a house that was very lonely. There were just the two of us. It was quite dark, and we did not have any of the things that people take for granted nowadays.

The uncle had a share in a restaurant in Merritt. He would come out maybe one month a year to be with us. These were quite joyous times, but when he left things were quite dull for a young child. I was quite active and an inquisitive person.

By the time I turned six, the whole world opened up to me because I went to grade school and learned English. All of a sudden I had friends. The neighbors were kids, and I had friends at school, and I knew a different language. The whole world expanded.

But it got to the point that I was so hypnotized by the outside world that I didn't want to go back home. I would go next door, and they were watching television, a Mickey Mouse show. These guys had toys, they had things to play with. I didn't have any of that stuff. For me it was an occasional comic book or whatever I could get hold of.

I assume you still spoke Chinese.

Yes, I spoke Cantonese, a dialect. We started having problems, because I would come home later and later, and she would threaten not to let me in. Finally she just locked the doors, and I stayed out fairly late, as a punishment. But in between that, we started having cultural problems. One time she asked me to go down to the meat market, and she wanted me to translate because I spoke English. I got this view of the butcher looming over the counter, looking at me and saying, "Look, kid, what does your grandma want?" I felt so

embarrassed by somebody telling me I should talk some language to
somebody else.

All of a sudden I realized I was quite different from everybody.
Because, up to that point, I felt I was just like any kid. There was no
colour, there was no, "We are different."

I was not coming home, I was not listening, I was not an
obedient child. One time she got so fed up with me that she took
me downstairs into the basement, tied me to one of the posts, went
upstairs and turned the lights off.

Very trying experience.

For me it was. At that point the family decided to get together, all the
different relatives, to discuss my future.

What age were you then?

I was about eight. The decision was to send me back to Hong Kong
"to get some culture" and for somebody to teach me properly and
get the wildness out of me. They bought me a ticket, unbeknownst
to me. At that point she was starting to prepare me for this experience and began to tell me that she was not my mother, that
there was this other person who was my mother and that she was
somewhere else. I could not comprehend that.

It was the beginning of having perception problems with the
world, and what was going on. What compounded this more was that
I had no way to let it out, so I went to my closest friends who were my
neighbors and said, "Gee, my mom says she is not my mom."

Of course they told their parents, and the parents got in touch
with the immigration office. They came and had a talk with us.
There wasn't any evidence. I was assuming another identity. My
name was Wong instead of Chu. My family name in Hong Kong is
Chu. So, as far as they were concerned, this kid was just exaggerat-
ing, talking gibberish. It caused enough of an alarm that they (the
family) decided they had to send me off.

So they dressed me up in my little suit with a little bow tie and
took me to the airport. They sewed my Chinese name onto the
jacket pocket of the vest and put me on the plane. One of the
stewardesses took care of me. I saw everybody on the ground waving
at me while I was taking off.

The next thing I knew I was in Hong Kong, stepping off the plane, and there were these people running at me. These two grown-up men. One of them grabbed me. He was excited and said, "You know who I am? I'm your father, and this is your uncle." I was taken home where I discovered I was supposed to have a whole slew of brothers and sisters, at least a half a dozen more.

But to me it was a make-believe family. I had a mother and a father, and I no longer understood what this really meant. Somehow, all I knew was that I did not belong here and that someday I would return to where I was supposed to be. That was how I coped with this idea of the family. I always felt as an outsider. But I coped. Here I was, supposed to be in the third grade in grade school in Canada, with no word of Chinese, nothing in the background.

You didn't speak Chinese? Really?

Well, I spoke a dialect. Hong Kong is a completely different dialect. I was more versed in English. So here I start from scratch. They gave me an ink brush, and I tried to colour in the ink spots to try and create the characters. I automatically was jumped a few grades to get up there. I managed to do very well. I was quite bright and caught on to what was going on. I managed to finish grade five. A few years down the road, my English was getting very rusty.

Overseas (back in Canada) there was apparently another (family) huddle going on, and they figured it was time to send me back.

What age were you then?

Twelve going on thirteen. The major reason I had to come back was that as soon as I turned thirteen, I was a full fare. So that mattered quite a bit, and of course all the other relatives got together and said, "Well, we can't waste this paper, and he seems to be doing quite well in Hong Kong now. We think it is time he was sent back over here." So a decision was made to repatriate me.

It was very lucky for me. I had a peek at grade six (in Hong Kong), and it was horrendous. We had to memorize by rote and recite. That was how the learning process was.

I was put onto a ship, again on my own. This was a funny thing. I had to go through immigration, and the immigration (officers) apparently did not believe that I was the same person (as described in his passport). So they decided to do a little test. Because most of the immigration people were Chinese, they looked at me and they looked at the picture, and of course I had changed quite a bit. They would say, "Well we're not sure about this guy." They decided to take me into the counsellor's office.

He was a full-blooded Canadian and spoke only English to me. He told me to sign this, and of course I understood everything, so I passed it. That saved my rump. Otherwise I would have been stuck in Hong Kong forever. I came back over here, and you have to understand that I was twelve or thirteen, too old for grade three anymore, so they jumped me to grade five.

So I was behind and, at the same time, I had to cope again. My studies have always been behind, and that is the reason why I never completed my high school. Everything was so mixed up. But what saved me was that rote memory that we learned in the Hong Kong school system. In the schools here most high school teachers will test you on what you remember, rather than on the course. So you figure out the system.

So you got good grades this way?

I was a B-average student. Then I spent a few years in the (British Columbia) interior in Merritt, because when I came back, my uncle—who I thought was my benefactor and the one whom I really revered—had had a series of strokes and he no longer could work in Merritt.

So, at thirteen years I was shifted to this little small town. There was a café, so I went with the Chinese café experience, which is what a lot of Chinese do.

I peeled one hundred fifty pounds of potatoes a day when I came back from school. A bit of your childhood gets lost that way, and I think a lot of Chinese kids my age, who grew up during the time I grew up, have probably had the same. In order for the family business to save money and make a go of it, everybody had to pitch in. So, I would go to school and I would come back at lunchtime and eat in the café, then I would wash some dishes and go back to school, come back later on after school, grab something to eat, and peeling potatoes until seven o'clock. I used to be able to peel a potato without looking at it, I was so good at it.

At that time I started to cultivate a very fertile imagination. I always had it, but the monotony of this kind of ritual started me having all these thoughts and ideas and imaginations. But you see, this period was psychologically very damaging, because I realized I was an illegal immigrant. I was living somebody else's life; I was living a borrowed life.

You still were?

Yes, until I was twenty-two. When I came back to Canada I had to fend for myself, so I felt more isolation. Immigrants always feel isolation, but I had a double whammy on me. When I went to Merritt, most of the people—besides the hired help—were all relatives. Every once in a while somebody would decide to discipline me or make it their duty to make sure I grew up properly. So I would be mistreated in some way, verbally and sometimes physically, being whacked a few times. It caused quite a bit of anger and hostility in me because I didn't understand.

Most people have a family. They have some shelter, some point of refuge that they can always go back to when the world collapses. For children there are always times when the world seems to be gone, and they will cry and have a secret place. A home, a room, or somewhere to feel safe. I never had that. What it did for me was it cultivated incredible survival instincts because I had to. I made it a point of making sure that whatever I did, whatever mistakes I committed, I would never make the same mistake again, because every mistake is fatal. The mistakes were from within and from without. It inhibited me in many ways. Socially, I was afraid of making close friends with schoolmates and with people I felt close to. Once they got too close I would start to back off. I was afraid they would find out that I was not who I was supposed to be—that would be a bad thing.

I didn't understand why I was sent to a place I didn't care about. I would get angry. Kids will get into fights. I would always have to contain myself and pull back. It was frustrating, because the more visible I became, the more afraid I became that I would be discovered.

You were afraid of being sent back, then, as a consequence of something?

Yes. I felt all the time that this was where I really belonged. So all these things were hanging over (me). I always felt that this whole place was a stage setting. For some reason some people disappear and go behind the scene or go up top somewhere, and through some peepholes they will be manipulating and creating things. You were supposed to act like you didn't know what was going on, like you hadn't caught on to it.

It seems like the gods were making these tests, letting these role-settings and strings hang over you. Of course that does a lot to your thinking as you turn into a writer. During this period I developed, but at the same time I was getting very depressed, and repression created a lot of difficulties. You got so angry that your emotions just shook and you have no control over yourself. There were so many of these conflicting things holding you back and pushing you forward. As the relatives started putting pressure on me, I became quite angry with the situation without understanding the whole phenomenon of the anger.

By then you were a teenager?

By that time I was a teenager. Eventually I had to lash back. Of course, the whole spectre of myself being a bad boy came up again. The relatives got together, had a big meeting, and their choice was to send me back, or whatever. My (real) mom, who was in Hong Kong, had a sister in Chicago, so she wrote and begged her to take me in. So, my aunt said okay. These guys just took me across the border by car, without going through any immigration procedures, and put me on a train.

Here I was, in Chicago, knowing I was illegal there. By that time I was quite clear, obviously I had no papers.

What year are we talking about?

The early sixties. I stayed there for three years. That period of my life was a strained one for another reason. My aunt owned a restaurant, and the only way I could make my keep was to work in the restaurant. My working condition was quite intensive. You went down there and you worked. Then my cousin, my aunt's son, decided to start a take-out delivery business, and I had to pitch in much harder.

The part of Chicago we were in was the old part of Chinatown. The new Chinatown moved, and the old part of Chinatown was just right on the edge of the Chicago Loop. It was quite run down. My aunt, ingeniously enough, decided that since Chinese food might no longer do it, she changed and became a Filipino-Chinese-Thai restaurant. Filipino nurses would come in and eat.

My studies were starting to catch up on me because you can only rely on rote for so long. When I graduated out of grade school I went into high school, one of the most prestigious Catholic private high schools in Chicago. The system they worked on was a kiss of death for me. So I asked the cousin to let me off because my grades were starting to decline, and I really had to work. He made certain promises too, but he didn't fulfill them at that point, and all hell started breaking loose.

Meanwhile this friend of mine, Jack, whom I had grown up with, was in Merritt all this time.

He is also Chinese?

Yes. He came to Chicago to visit me. He said, "Look, things have changed in Merritt. They are starting to pay you a dollar an hour. You do get paid for your work, and you have so much more freedom. So, if you don't like it, you can always go back." That gave me an escape route.

But at the same time this woman came into my life. I was seventeen. She taught me a little more about love and things like that. I would almost say she seduced me. But the thing that I was starting to be aware of was that that she liked Chinese things. I happened to be Chinese. She said that she was going to work and support me through high school. I was totally confused because too many things were problematic. One, I was an illegal immigrant. I didn't know if I could explain that to her, or what would happen. I also had such pressure at work and with my family there. Things came to a point where I figured, "Hey, is this what I want for the rest of my life?" So I wrote her a letter and dropped it in her mailbox.

Then I went back to the family and said I was leaving. I had made a decision. That was incredible for me, to be able to make a decision. I was feeling terrible about it, because it seemed I was the only one who was really helping my aunt, understanding her.

So I went back to Merritt. I worked there for a little while. I started making friends again—Japanese brothers, Danny and Andrew. We stuck together as buddies. We drove a car down the main drag at ninety miles an hour, not getting caught, and things like that.

The unfortunate thing about working in the restaurant after school was that, as the waiter, you would end up taking a lot of flak from your schoolmates. Of course when the good-looking girls came in, you got butterflies and got embarrassed because you were serving people. It is a very subservient attitude (situation) which didn't help me mentally.

Eventually I decided that I wanted to make a break from that situation. So Andy and I took off. We spent about four months in the Okanagan picking fruit. In November it got too cold, and there wasn't enough work, and so I went back to high school. (But after a while,) I looked at myself and said, "This is not working. There are so many obstacles and this principal, he just absolutely hates me and just wants me out of this place."

A year earlier, Jack had left and gone to Vanderhoof, a little town out of Prince George. He had a friend or relative there who opened a little Chinese drive-in restaurant. He seemed to be doing fairly well, and I figured I would go and work for him. I managed to make it up to Prince George, went to Vanderhoof and found him. His boss was quite nice. He said, "I can't put you here, we don't need another person yet, but I know somebody in Prince George who needs a waiter." So, I was lucky I was trained in the restaurant business, at least I could survive.

You were then eighteen?

I was eighteen or nineteen by that time. I stayed in Prince George for three years. I tried to grow a moustache to look older, smoked a pipe, and tried to hang around to learn about what life was all about. I started hearing about all these things when I came down to Vancouver once in a while—all these stories that they had spies up there, giving my aunt all this information that I was married to this Indian woman, and I was having this and that, and I was a total disgrace to any respectable Chinese.

What drove me to come down was that I met a girl up there. She was very, very kind-hearted and a very warm type of person. But what really got me hooked into it was when I saw her family. They were not rich, but it was a very together, warm family, something I never had. I wanted it so badly that I made myself fall in love with this girl, and when it didn't work out I was totally broken and drifted down to Vancouver. I spent a year in Vancouver.

When did you come down to Vancouver?

It was about 1969 or 1970. During the hippy times. I have been in Vancouver for about fifteen years now.

When did you first start writing, and how did that happen?

The reason why I couldn't write to that point was that I felt it was not really my forte; although I was thoroughly Canadianized, there was a part of me that was very Chinese.

At that time, I was very very angry, a lot of self-pity, wrapping myself up with a lot of frustrations that I didn't understand. I knew that I could turn one way or the other, that I could be a really bad character, or I had to channel the anger somehow. Jack was in Vancouver at that time with a group of friends with whom we hung around together. We were just like a rat pack.

How good was your Chinese then?

I forgot (it) all. In ten years I lost it. If I looked at a newspaper I could comprehend it, but my tongue was so raw that I couldn't speak it. It was so frustrating. At the same time I met a group of Chinese who were related to me. That was in San Francisco. I made friends and started going up and down the coast. I saw they were more into community and more into things, so when I came back up here to Vancouver I decided to volunteer my time.

I made a choice that I was going to channel my energies into something useful. I went into the community. The other reason was that I wanted my language back. I went into the Pender YWCA in Vancouver, in Chinatown, and I volunteered.

I would fill out forms for old people, and they would converse with me. I would make an exchange with them. What services I needed they would do. These old people are so isolated themselves that they wanted someone to listen to them. After they found a willing ear, through sheer force of energy they just hung onto you, and their whole life stories just poured out.

The bitterness, the pain and all of it. I started to realize that, "Gee, I am not the only guy who is having a rough time. These guys are having the same," and so I started getting more involved with the history of China(town) and put it all together. That started my search into the phenomenon of why we were what we were, and then, the more I researched, the more I realized that I was not isolated, I was not going through hell by myself. In fact, I think at that time probably one in three Chinese in Vancouver or Canada were probably going through the same phenomenon.

As I dug deeper I realized the legislations and what caused the victimization. Some of these people actually kept secret their identity and brought it to the grave with them. But the family, the healthy families would know nothing about it. So I was just part of one phenomenon, and that helped me. It started opening me up to what was going on.

From there, I went to the art school, and I used photography as a means to communicate with people. I took portraits in Chinatown. But it lacked something because I felt I could not communicate all the things that I wanted to say.

With every person I photographed I wanted to make sure I knew something about them. After a while I knew too much. When you put the photograph on the wall it doesn't say what it wants to say, so I knew I had to take another step.

So I went into radio, and at the same time a group of us kids got together and produced the first radio program on *Pender Guy* (broadcast on Co-op Radio, Vancouver). I spent five or six years developing that. It was a search for me. A search to find another way to communicate what I couldn't express in a visual form. The reason why I couldn't write up to that point was that I felt it was (not) really my forte. Although I was thoroughly Canadianized there was a part of me that was very very Chinese.

I feel sometime more precise in the Chinese language. I am a bilingual person, and English is in fact my second language. Through all this mess of schooling, I never really had proper training, although English was a subject that I relished. I love history and stories. I felt I was inadequate. I didn't feel I could go through

English. I didn't feel that I could write properly, and I didn't even feel I could communicate properly.

So I learned from the outside, learning in, rather than a lot of people learning through the school system going out. So every step I took was very painful. Finally I realized that I had so many stories about so many people that the stories would die with me.

I felt I had to write them, I had to put them down. I had to make them real, maybe release them from their miseries. I was very active in the Chinese community. Up to that point I had been a bit of a rabble-rouser and an activist. For me it was trying to find the truth in matters, and you find that the community is very polarized, it is not as homogeneous as everybody thinks.

You were trying to write?

Well, I needed grammar. I needed very rudimentary things. I can compose. I can put together things. I was writing scripts for the radio program. I mean there was no problem of putting together complex things, except I was murdering the language, and it was something I went through. I was a grown-up student by then. I had to go through this whole rigmarole with community college.

I took some English courses and from there I managed somehow to wheedle my way into university and taking only creative writing courses, because this was the only course I felt gave me things, (but) even in creative writing they dealt with the craft but not the rudimentaries.

They assumed that you knew the basics.

Yes, for me it was hard. For me writing is a very difficult experience. It is a painful experience because of my lack of form and language. When I try to write, I often try to compose on the typewriter because my hand-writing is so poor. But, when I compose on the typewriter, often enough I correct myself as I go along, and it just gets in the way of the thought. So I was having incredible difficulties working with the language.

Of course, when I went to the creative writing course, most of the people there are either in the business or taking it for some other reason. They had formidable backgrounds compared to me. I just felt like saying, "Gee, how can I deal with it?" Except that I had all the life experiences behind me, and for me the important thing was to figure out what this whole writing thing was about and to find the measuring sticks—what was good writing, and why some writings exist even two or three hundred years after the author is dead—what is significant about it? (I wanted) to understand what it is and to try to relate and work in the same way.

When I walked into a group of old people, I instantly got into conversation because I knew their life stories. I knew more, sometimes, about the history and where they stood than they did. They knew the stories, they knew the people, but I knew where they were. And so, after a while, I felt very comfortable with them. That is how much knowledge and experience I brought with me. At one point a group of people in the community got together and created an anthology.

We did everything wrong. We did six hundred copies and terrible marketing and never got rid of it. Right now it is a collector's item, but there was enough in there that triggered things off for me, and I carried it through. What started me to write, essentially, like most other writers, were things that happened in the past.

And what was happening was that I had these buttons in me that were getting pushed constantly. I couldn't understand why I always averted my eyes and felt humble and little in front of somebody who had any kind of authority over me, even though they were wrong. I could not speak for myself. I knew there were all these ghosts in my past that kept recurring, and I felt I had to deal with it if I wanted to be a whole person.

So you built this up and built it up to a certain point where I woke up one night and took a pen and wrote.

Can you remember when that was?

It was probably when I was about twenty-four or twenty-five. The words were plain but incredibly powerful. The energy, the concentration, the stories I wrote. The stories were so strong that I could not write them in my own person. I made up a character, Little Chu. I had to write it in another form to see it. I wrote out all these things that bothered me. I just wanted to get it out of my system. It took me a long time after that to even look at it because there was so much uncertainty and so much fear about it.

Finally when I did look at it, it started to untie the knots, all the things that were inside of me started to clear up a lot more. My aunt, I (really) saw her for the first time. Because all I saw was the experiences of the pain and all that. Now I saw beyond that. Now I saw it in actuality, that we were victimizing each other without realizing how the other person felt and not knowing or understanding where the other person was from. We were both trying to deal with the life we were given in the best way possible. Although I still don't get along with my aunt, I have a whole different sense and value for her.

And that was the time when things came full circle. I began to create a new adjustment to it. That helped. The experiences of writing became very important. But that did not become valuable until I started reciting some of this to some friends. All of a sudden, when I was reciting it, it evoked so many powerful feelings inside that they started reciting their stories, telling me what happened to them.

But I still didn't see myself as a writer. Through the radio program, we took a grant and went to the Interior to document some of the Chinese communities there. I went into Kamloops, which is about sixty miles north of Merritt, and there was only one Chinese Association building left. Chinatown was getting demolished, and there was nothing left anymore. This old man was doing the caretaking.

I said, "Look, I want to take you to the Chinese cemetery." So we drove up to this place, but nothing in my experience had prepared me for what I was going to see. I know what cemeteries are like, but I went to this place, and it was the most forlorn and sad hunk of hilly gravel. There was nothing there. Hunks of decaying wood. The only thing that resembled a grave stone was a slab of concrete on which, before it was set, somebody had scribbled the person's name on it.

This was the old Chinese cemetery. There is a new Chinese cemetery, but the old Chinese cemetery was where all the railway workers and all the people who died and had no place to go and nobody to look after them, that was where they were buried. Subsequently, some of the bones were retrieved and sent back to China so there were big mounds left.

I came back to Vancouver, and even after two or three weeks the experience still bothered me. One night I got up and wrote and showed it to some people. I said, "Hey this is a poem." So I became a poet.

How old were you then?

Almost thirty, I guess.

And that is what you have been writing since? Poems?

I have been writing since and published by fluke. My life has always been a series of flukes and providence. My poetry was in fact paintings. They had depth, they had the whole background, and they had such an impact. At the same time it was very simple because the influence of my writing is partly from the Chinese part of it. Very simple, very stark and with very austere words, but fully packed. Every word has to have its own weight and its own feeling. There is no waste of words.

As in Haiku?

In that similar form, but mine was very readable. I wanted it to be very common so that anybody can look at it, read it, and understand it. My most rewarding experience was actually having this neighbor's son, about nine or eleven years old—he loved it. He recited some of my poetry to his class. They loved it. But for him to understand it and relate to it was something I really wanted. Because for me, some of the writing was like jumping through literary hoops. This was valid writing.

To me it is important that I tell stories. I was using it as a medium to relate the experience and the emotional quality of things.

The reason I write poetry is I don't have enough emotional facilities together at this point even to write full stories. My grammar is still terrible. For a long time, one of the problems for me was that I felt I could not communicate.

Did you legalize yourself at any point?

When I turned twenty-two. I finally said, "Okay, I will give it a crack." But the legalizing process caused a problem because I was quite well known in the community already. I was known as Jim Wong.

And here I was going to change my name. Now it created a lot of problems. After a long search of how I was going to do it, I was going to join the two names together and hyphenate them so that if I had descendants, I would start my own dynasty.

I am working on an anthology now. The anthology of Chinese-Canadian writing, and that project is based on an analysis of the earliest time I was interested in history. It was very important. Until the sixties and seventies nobody recognized it. The only book written was totally inaccurate, but it was well-meant. When we worked on the radio station I was amassing incredible amounts of documenting material. We had to start legitimizing the history and finally the books, the academic books, were published and people began accepting that there was a history (of Chinatown).

I looked into that history, and all it was was references from newspapers. Bare, bare bones. Essentially a skeleton with no flesh and no life to it.

Then this whole idea of culture came about because at one time somebody at one of these community meetings got up and said, "Look, I like culture, and don't get me wrong, but I don't believe the Chinese in Canada have culture. They don't have any art, they don't have any literature, they don't have any music that is Chinese-Canadian. Well, I'd like to see it, but it is not there."

I was very angry, but at the same time I could not argue because I could not articulate that. But I kept it in me. I said, "Son of a bitch, I am going to prove it." So I had to define what that culture was. For me, then, it was like taking the whole phenomenon and looking at it and saying no.

The culture itself is not the art. That is only a manifestation. The literature is only a manifestation of it. The culture itself is the thought and that thought of culture started when the first Chinese stepped into Canada and started thinking of themselves as Canadian, "I have to look and I have to survive, and I have to look at my life here."

That is the Chinese-Canadian culture—as old as the first Chinese who stepped off (the ship). That is what culture is. But in the same way we had to express it. So now that the history was built, we had to develop the other aspects of the manifest culture which is the performing arts and the literature.

The anthology is a very ambitious project to legitimize the

literary arts of Chinese in Canada. We are searching as far back as we can because a lot of the writing was done in Chinese in the past. What we see now is very superficial. And the reason why that all started is that when I published my book, I found out this was the first book published by a Chinese-Canadian with poems about Chinatown. This is in the eighties, and finally this came out. So, I felt I have to bring the whole thing with me. Then, the anthology. That is why.

JURGEN HESSE is a writer and editor with four previous books to his credit: *The Story of ACTRA* (Thinkware, 1985), *The Radio Documentary Handbook* (Self-Counsel, 1987), *Mobile Retirement Handbook* (Self-Counsel, 1987), and *Tips and Tools for Better Writing* (Thinkware, 1988). He has also written regularly for the *Vancouver Sun* and *Toronto Globe & Mail,* and produced radio documentaries for the CBC. He lives in White Rock, B.C.